All On The Line

Pádraic Maher is a Tipperary hurler who has won three All-Ireland titles, five Munster championships and six All-Star awards, as well as seven Tipperary county senior hurling titles with his beloved Thurles Sarsfields. He announced his retirement from hurling in 2022 having appeared over 130 times in the blue and gold of Tipperary in league and championship as a first-choice defender for the county for 13 years. A garda based in Limerick, Pádraic also co-owns Heyday Coffee House in Thurles with Tipperary team-mate Seamus Callanan.

All On The Line

A memoir of hurling and commitment

Pádraic Maher

HACHETTE
BOOKS
IRELAND

Copyright © 2022 Pádraic Maher

The right of Pádraic Maher to be identified as the author of
the work has been asserted by him in accordance with the
Copyright, Designs and Patents Act 1988.

First published in Ireland in 2022 by
HACHETTE BOOKS IRELAND

First published in paperback in 2023

1

Cataloguing in Publication Data is available from the British Library

ISBN 9781399714105

Typeset in Adobe Garamond Pro by Bookends Publishing Services, Dublin
Printed and bound in Great Britain by Clays Ltd, Elcograf, S.p.A.

Hachette Books Ireland policy is to use papers that are natural, renewable
and recyclable products and made from wood grown in sustainable forests.
The logging and manufacturing processes are expected to conform to the
environmental regulations of the country of origin.

Hachette Books Ireland
8 Castlecourt Centre
Castleknock
Dublin 15, Ireland

A division of Hachette UK Ltd
Carmelite House, 50 Victoria Embankment, EC4Y 0DZ

www.hachettebooksireland.ie

For my mam Helen, my dad Paddy, my brother Ronan
and my fiancée Claire – the people who
are always in my corner

Contents

With thanks to Michael Moynihan
for his help in writing this book

Prologue

'I think I'm done.'

This is how a career ends. Not at the end of an All-Ireland final with the Liam MacCarthy Cup in your hands. Not with a realisation in the dressing room after club training.

No, my career came to an end in an office in Limerick on an ordinary street, in the middle of an ordinary afternoon, on the way to my engagement party with Claire, my fiancée. I was seeing a specialist in an attempt to get to the bottom of some dizzy spells and blurred vision which affected me at the tail end of the 2021 club season, and he laid it on the line: I'd damaged a neck artery and that was giving me mini-strokes. A serious collision or impact on the field of play … He couldn't tell me to stop playing but that if I were his son or his brother, that would be his advice.

I went outside and rang my mother, and that was my opening line: 'I think I'm done.' I rang Claire and told her the same. Tough phone calls on a tough day.

After the shock wore off I got a second opinion, and a third, and they were consistent. After a whole life revolving around hurling, it was over.

That's not how I wanted it to end. I felt I had a couple of good years in me with Tipperary and Thurles Sarsfields, was feeling as fit and hungry as ever, and I was keen to support my brother Ronan as he captained the county, but it wasn't to be.

As time has passed I've tried to make my peace with retirement. It's not always easy. People looking at me might think that life is good: I'm engaged to be married, I've got the coffee shop and a great job, but a huge part of my life was taken away suddenly and I've found it, mentally, very hard. At times it's a struggle, and I hope to make my peace with it sooner rather than later, but at least I am able to look back and enjoy my career, and to appreciate the memories and the friendships I have made in my club and county. I can acknowledge the absolute privilege it has been to wear the blue and gold jersey of Tipperary and Thurles Sarsfields' blue and white – and the challenge of fitting a life in around those commitments.

This is my story. And just like on those big days in Semple Stadium or Croke Park, I hope I have left it all out there.

Early days in Tonagha

We're all Thurles people. My father's side of the family all come from Mullaunbrack, out by Killinan, the hill near the graveyard as you drive into Thurles past the racecourse. That's where they were all reared. His uncle was the great John Maher – my granduncle – from the bottom of Killinan Hill. My mother's family is McCormack, they're all from Archestown, you go out the Dublin road and make a right turn and it's two or three miles down that road.

They're bordering the parish of Moycarkey-Borris, so over the years my uncles on Mam's side, Paddy and Maurice McCormack, would have wondered if they should have played with Moycarkey-Borris, but that was never going to happen. Or at least they didn't wonder too hard, put it that way, but we're still maybe 500 yards from Moycarkey territory.

Having said all that, I put down a few years in Loughmore-Castleiney when I was very small. My parents got married in 1987 and – why, I don't know – they bought a house out in Clondoty in Loughmore, a mile from the village. I was born in 1989 so I gave the first five years of my life out there; they didn't come back straight away either. There's a yarn they tell about the local parish priest approaching my father while I was still a baby, and saying I'd have to get baptised in Loughmore.

'That young lad will be baptised in Thurles,' said my father, pointing down at me in the pram.

No more conversation about baptisms in Loughmore. There was a bit of a backstory involving my father having some disagreements with the priest, but not on matters of doctrine – on the hurling field.

They built a house in Tonagha which is in the countryside outside Thurles, and that's where I grew up. It was a country upbringing, really; if I looked to go into town as a small child my parents would be looking at me: 'What do you want to go into town for?' would be the reaction.

We grew up in green fields, surrounded by farms, my grandmother Josie a couple of hundred yards down the road, and that was our world. My cousins Patrick and Barry, on my mother's side, lived nearby, and we all hung around together, Barry and I are roughly the same age. The only reason to go to town was for school Monday to Friday and hurling in Dúrlas Óg on a Saturday morning. All things considered, I wouldn't class myself as a townie, even though I live in town myself now and love it there.

There were plenty of kids around the place older than us and younger than us, and we knocked around together. Sometimes we'd have a 'war' with another group, two tribes taking each other on in the woods by throwing stones or some other messing, which got hairy enough until we were old enough to have sense.

My father was working for Telecom Éireann then. He'd be working above in Naas or Kildare, gone at six in the morning and not back until seven at night (no motorways to shorten the journey that time) and my mother was working in Moloughney's, a TV shop in Thurles, so she was in and out of town, but we weren't. We were happy enough out in Tonagha having our battles in the woods, our nanny, Josie, looking after us. And playing hurling.

As soon as we could walk we got a hurley, so it was always in my hand. Walking around at home, going over the fields to visit people, I always had the hurley, pucking a sliotar ahead of me or hitting it off a wall.

On top of that my father was still playing for Thurles Sarsfields at the time, when I was four or five. He'd have been going into training with the club so I'd jump into the car, and while they were playing backs and forwards or running their laps, I'd be flying around the field myself. Even when my father called it a day I still ended up going to see the Sarsfields train. My uncle Paddy was over the team and he lived right next door to us, so every Friday evening I'd head in with him, myself and a couple of cousins: 'Go on, get into the van, there's training.'

And there was a financial incentive as well. After training we'd be given five quid to collect every hurling ball that had gone behind the goals. That was the pitch outside Semple Stadium, which people will know from going through it to get to big games there. I got to know every inch of that field hunting out balls for Paddy. My cousins and I loved it – the trip in, the training, pucking around and hitting the ball back in from behind the goal.

Brendan Carroll was playing with the Sarsfields that time and he'd often take the old grip off his hurley and roll it into a ball and throw it to me or one of the other lads, and we'd be delighted. Heaven. Bring the grip home and put it on my own hurley, which was so small then that it was mostly grip I ended up playing with because I was wrapping the entire hurley in it.

Because of all that, we'd be upset if we missed a session. If my mother brought me out somewhere on a Friday evening and we got back late, and Paddy's van wasn't there … disaster. I'd be thinking, 'He didn't wait for me.' Most of the time he'd hang on, though. Tuesday nights could be touch and go for us, with school the following morning there was no guarantee you'd be allowed go, but most Fridays we were there. The other side of it was that if he and the selectors had a meeting, you had to wait around until he was finished. But sometimes that meant you were there when they were picking the team for a game. You ended up knowing the team before the players did.

I started going up to Dúrlas Óg for under-6 training, the parents dropping me in. Naturally enough, there were a few Saturday mornings at nine o'clock when I needed to be convinced to get into the car; there might have been a cartoon on the television I was more interested in and I'd kick up a fuss, but once we got going I was grand. (People may be confused by the fact that I played for Dúrlas Óg as a kid but Thurles Sarsfields later. In the late 1970s, Dúrlas Óg was established as a separate underage club which practically every youngster in the town went to up to the age of 16. Most kids would go from Dúrlas Óg on to the Sarsfields from minor up, as I did.)

Setbacks and surprises: a hurling apprenticeship

Hurling went to another level when I started in primary school in Scoil Ailbhe, which is by the railway tracks on the way up to Semple Stadium. In terms of the game I had it quick enough anyway, I suppose, but in the school hurling was taken very seriously. There were 'yard leagues', and I'd often be made captain of one of the school teams in fourth and fifth class, so I knew I had something to offer.

And that in turn made me more interested in Dúrlas Óg. I'd be pucking around in school during the week, then when I fell in with Dúrlas Óg on a Saturday morning I was looking forward to it and getting the benefit of it. So as I got a bit older I took it more seriously because I was enjoying it.

The school had teams at under-11 and under-13 (in football and hurling), playing in the A grade in Cumann na mBunscoil, the primary schools' competition, and we reached county finals a few times.

The county final was an occasion. We were up against a school from Carrick-on-Suir at under-11s one year, and we also had great battles with St Peter and Paul's of Clonmel – two big towns. The Carrick final was played in Semple Stadium, but the build-up started at the school.

The day of the game, the school basically shut down. Everyone was dressed up in the school colours, black and red, and there were songs all morning, the atmosphere getting hotter until the players got called out of the classrooms. Then, because the school is so close to the stadium, we all walked up together to Semple, still chanting, still singing – like a tribe going to war, marching up to battle.

We won the Carrick final which was fantastic, not only for the sense of elation at the time, but because it also gave us a taste of what it's like to win a game in Semple Stadium. The stands were echoing and the terraces empty, but you can feel the power of the place, the history that gives it an aura. That was a special moment for me and, young as I was, I knew it.

We had a good team. Michael Gleeson, one of my best friends, would go on to hurl for the Sarsfields for years and win an All-Ireland minor with Tipp, was on it as well. We also won the under-13 final a couple of years later.

There were other little touches that impressed the importance of the game on us. For instance, the school principal, Flan Quigney, got the hurleys for school from Delaneys down in Kilkenny, and he kept them in a big bin in his office. If you broke your hurley playing a match then it was like Christmas heading into school the morning afterwards. My mother would give me the price of the hurley and in class I'd say to the teacher I had to get a new hurley – the first order of business, before she even had her coat off. Then down to the principal's office, waiting outside for him to arrive in, and when he came he'd show you the bin: 'Take whatever suits you.'

I can remember sitting outside the office, knocking on the door ... there was a nervousness involved, going in to pick out the hurley I would use for the next few months. Then back to the classroom with it, happy as Larry, looking at it all day, mad to get home and try it out. It's the small things that keep us happy, after all.

The teachers in Scoil Ailbhe were a huge influence on all of us. Fergal O'Reilly was one, an Arravale Rovers man from Tipperary Town, while Donal Ryan and Denis McCullagh from Holycross-Ballycahill were other teachers who drove it. None of them involved in Thurles clubs, incidentally, but they did a lot for Gaelic games in the town. They would have played a big part in keeping us going to Dúrlas Óg, for instance, where we were able to show the benefit of the coaching and preparation with the school – all the basics, including rising the ball, striking, hooking, blocking. Dúrlas Óg ran street leagues, dividing the town into teams: 'Tipperary', 'Cork', 'Clare' and so on, and you got a sense of how you were going from those street league games.

I play left hand on top – always did, from the day I picked up a hurley. I'm naturally left-handed and write with my left hand, so when a priest in school tried to get me to switch to right hand on top it didn't work out for either of us and I went back to what I knew.

My father was coming to the end of his career when I started going along to the games. I was pretty young – around six or seven years of age – and probably didn't take it in. I can remember one game when he was in the half-forward line and my uncles Maurice (on my mother's side) and Connie (on my father's side) were in the half-forward line with him. The Sarsfields' supporters called that line 'the iron curtain' because the ball wouldn't get past them into the full-forward line, they'd stop it every time.

Although I have a memory of the three of them playing – and Paddy, another uncle, in goal – not many details of those games come to mind, though I've seen videos since then. The games I do remember include four county finals in a row they played in with the Sarsfields, my uncle and godfather Connie featuring, but they lost the four of them. For a couple of those I was a water boy, so there are clearer memories of those ones in particular, and of them winning divisional titles like the Mid-Tipp finals, which was a major deal then for the club. Nowadays you'd ask lads how many county medals they have, but then it was a matter of fellas having four 'Mid' medals while a county championship was out of reach.

Losing those county finals was heartbreaking. I can remember crying at the final whistle a couple of times, walking out onto the field and seeing the likes of my father or my uncle Connie, devastated.

Connie's last ever match was one of those county finals. I have a distinct memory of seeing him walk up to my uncle Paddy, as I was in tears out on the field.

After losing four finals in a row they were shattered, and

the usual rigmarole followed those games. They'd be on the beer for a couple of days drowning their sorrows (something I paid no heed to until ten years later when I was doing it myself). They came very, very close a couple of times. In the 2002 final they were up against a good Mullinahone side, with John Leahy and the two Kellys, Eoin and Paul. I was on water-boy duty again, blue and white colours around my head as I went up and down the sideline, and I can remember kneeling down to watch Leahy take a free to level the game.

He stuck it. Mullinahone won the replay.

I was getting a feel for the club and its history then. There might be 12,000 to 15,000 people at a county final, which drilled home how important the club was within the county. It's natural enough. Both sides of the family were interested in the game and both were blue and white to the core. I can remember my mother bringing me to club games in Littleton and other places, I'd stroll off down the sideline pucking a ball. I remember nothing about those games, but you're steeped in it all the time. You're at games, watching games, watching players.

There was a routine and a rhythm to many of our Sundays that a lot of people can probably remember. We'd all go to mass, and then my father might have a pint or two afterwards in the Sarsfields centre, with me alongside having a bottle of orange; it was a time when people could do that and still drive home for the dinner, which would usually be a roast. Then we'd head out to find a match in The Ragg or Borrisoleigh or wherever.

Sometimes we'd go a bit further. I can remember hopping in the car and heading off with my father to inter-county matches, in Cork in particular. It was a time when Tipp seemed to be playing Clare a lot in the Munster championship, so a lot of those games were playing in the old Páirc Uí Chaoimh. Those were days that would tell you there was something special about the game, starting with the journey. Before the motorway you could end up seeing a lot more of places like Fermoy than you really wanted to, with the traffic jams. It always seemed to be roasting hot, and sitting in the old uncovered stand in the Páirc you'd be looking out for the lad selling the ice cream out of the cardboard box.

Tipp would come out and the whole place – a full house, 40,000 people – would go mental. Then Clare would come out and they'd go mental all over again, and Davy Fitzgerald would sprint out across the field and wear the hurley off the crossbar ... the match itself didn't make as much of an impact as the surrounding spectacle, it was so full-on. I can remember being maybe seven years old, and the whole experience was nearly too much for me – the noise, the heat, the excitement, the stadium bouncing, almost. I had to burrow into my father to calm down, it was so overwhelming.

Not all of it was overwhelming, of course. My father would have parked the car on the Marina near one of the rowing clubs with the car facing for home for the quick getaway. And we'd always leave with a couple of minutes to go in order to beat the crowd. Win, lose or draw – an early exit.

In 1999 Clare were playing Tipperary and he gave me the elbow near the end of the game.

'Come on, we'll get going and beat the crowd.'

Tipp were leading by a couple of points, so he felt confident. We were heading down the river to get the car and we heard the roar.

'That's it now,' he said, 'They've won.'

Into the car. On with the radio: *Davy Fitzgerald's penalty has made this a dramatic draw* … Silence in the car until we stopped for chips in Fermoy.

By the age of 13 or 14 I was becoming more aware of the game. Aware that I was getting on the ball a good bit, playing centre-back or in some other central position. I was getting bigger and stronger, and I began to see the benefit of that in training and matches. My confidence too was building bit by bit, and by the time I started secondary school in Thurles CBS I felt I could hold my own in hurling.

Thurles CBS has a great hurling tradition, and the Harty Cup is the focus, as it is for all of the hurling schools in Munster. The last time Thurles won the Harty was back in 1956 with Jimmy Doyle, so that's the heritage. We started off with the Rice Cup, a schools' competition for under-14s (first and second years) and again, that was good for the confidence. The CBS wouldn't just have players in from the Sarsfields, there were also lads who played for Holycross-Ballycahill, for Moycarkey-Borris, for Moyne-Templetuohy, so there was a good pool of talent there. I made the team in 2002 as a 13-year-old in First Year, which was another indication that I was improving. We got to the Rice Cup final that year, against Callan CBS. The game was in Templemore, and there was an exciting build-up to it – a final, Kilkenny opposition, all of that – but we lost by a point. Devastation.

The whole approach to the game changes in secondary school. You're sitting next to fellas from different clubs and you get friendly with them, or you end up playing for the school with them. Then the summer holidays come and you're back playing against them for the club in the championship and trying to get one over on them.

The Dúrlas Óg team at that age group was good enough. We'd have won Mid-Tipp finals, divisional finals, but a good team from Nenagh used to beat us regularly in county finals. They had lads like Michael Heffernan and Paddy Murphy who would go on to play for Tipperary. They were our main rivals at underage level, and they beat us in an under-12 county final in Semple Stadium one year and did the same two years later in the under-14 county final, beating us that time by a point.

But we had the upper hand in the Féile na nGael, the national under-14 competition. I was on the age for our team. Michael Cahill, who hurled for Tipp for years, was on the team as well, and we won the 'Mid' final before beating Nenagh by six points in the county final. That was a big deal, and we knew it. The Féile is a highlight for thousands of kids, it's a big tournament and people take it very seriously. You end up representing your county, like in the All-Ireland club championships, and you'd often hear about some superstar or other that first caught people's eye in the Féile.

We went on to the All-Ireland series in Mullingar in 2003, and we'd heard about the last Dúrlas Óg team to

ALL ON THE LINE

win it back in 1990 with the likes of Johnny Enright and my cousin Mark King on the team. There was a group of four teams, with two to qualify for the latter stages. We lost to James Stephens of Kilkenny but still qualified to get out of the group. We rolled on through the quarter-final and the semi-final to get to the final, in the stadium in Mullingar. Again, there was the sense of a big occasion. We heard that busloads of supporters were coming up from Thurles for the game. They were to be disappointed, however, because we ended up getting beaten by James Stephens again. More heartbreak.

Between the Rice Cup, the county finals against Nenagh and that Féile na nGael final, there was plenty of disappointment to go around for me but, looking back now, I was learning my trade. The primary and secondary schools, and the club, were very good at building up those occasions. I'd have been very nervous going out to play in those matches, naturally enough, but like anything else, the more big games you play, the more you learn to deal with the anticipation and the pressure that goes with them. I was getting good experience with the school and the club, the games building gradually in intensity and importance.

Later on in my career I learned more about dealing

with those pressures, though you always have some sense of nervousness before a big game, no matter how experienced you are. But those finals were very important in exposing me, and other players, to the build-up to a big game and learning to perform in those games.

In school, for instance, even the photographs hanging on the walls of the corridors, of past teams, made you aware of the heritage. In conversation a teacher might say, 'Jimmy Doyle has a Rice Cup medal,' or 'Jimmy Doyle has a Dean Ryan Cup medal,' so that lesson was seeping in all the time. The irony, of course, was that Jimmy was also someone I saw at matches or even around the town. He was an icon, an immortal of the game, and also someone who could be sitting next to you in the Thurles Sarsfields Centre. Even if we were training later on as Sarsfields minors you could glance over and he'd be strolling past with his dog, so he was someone who was always around. A great, great player, but also someone who was part of the place.

The same with Mickey 'Rattler' Byrne. We used to take part in the St Patrick's Day parade with Dúrlas Óg, all of us in our gear parading behind the club banner. Mickey would hold one end of the banner and be roaring and talking to everyone in the town as we went along, telling jokes, knowing everyone, running the show basically.

That's part of the GAA. Until I was in my late teens I didn't realise who the man was I saw every weekend in Dúrlas Óg. 'Pat' was the fella at the front gate every Saturday morning, meeting kids and making them feel welcome. When I got older I learned he was Pat Stakelum, one of the greatest names in Tipperary hurling, who won All-Irelands with the county back in the 1950s.

I made good progress in school in hurling, and academically I was going ... very ordinary to be honest. But first year with the Rice Cup, losing in the final by a point. Second year in the Rice Cup we played Charleville in the final down in Tipp Town and they beat us in extra time by a point. Their star was Ryan Clifford, and that was the name we heard all the time: 'Mind Clifford, don't let Clifford get the ball.' But that was still two finals lost by a point.

We won the Croke Cup, which is a Tipperary-only schools competition, but we were also competing in the White Cup, a Munster schools competition, and eventually I made it to the Dean Ryan Cup team, another Munster schools competition. Serious stuff. That's an under-16-and-a-half competition – the Harty is under-19 – and you start coming up against the big powers, Flannan's and Colman's. One year Séamus Hickey, who had a great career with

Limerick, was on the Flannan's Dean Ryan team, and we heard he was on their Harty Cup team as well, which was a measure of a good player.

In my second year on the Dean Ryan, 2005, I made the Harty Cup team. I was 16, playing full-back. We beat Colman's in the semi-final, which was a big deal given their reputation. And a big deal given how long Thurles CBS had been without the Harty – going back to Jimmy Doyle's time in the fifties, as we often heard in the school. The final was against Flannan's, in Nenagh, and was built up like an All-Ireland.

They had a good team too. James McInerney and Colin Ryan, who played for Clare later, Séamus Hickey ... I was marking Bernard Gaffney, who would go on to play for Clare and win a couple of Fitzgibbon Cups. That was the first time I remember thinking the opposition were a serious, serious team. Gaffney would have been close to the age limit, a big man – a year makes a difference when you're playing that level. Nowadays a Harty player might have two or three years of gym work behind him, but not us. Not back then.

Flannan's beat us by five points, but we went through to the All-Ireland series, meeting St Kieran's College, Kilkenny. I ended up marking Richie Hogan, a man I met a good few times afterwards. They also had T.J. Reid and Paddy Hogan on the team. They beat us well, and that match really showed the level you had to reach, and what really good players were capable of. I had to remind myself that I was 16 and had a bit to go yet, and in fact I saw a lot of those Kilkenny lads again 12 months later in the All-Ireland minor semi-final, but that year really stood to me in terms of development. With Tipperary, that is. Not so much with the school competitions.

Looking forward to the 2006 Harty Cup campaign, we were confident. There were a good few who'd played in the previous year's final, and we had six or seven players in and around the Tipperary minor team – it was all looking good. We cruised through the group stages and were in good shape heading to Fermoy for the semi-final. We were playing Midleton CBS, who had future Cork seniors Paudie O'Sullivan at centre-back and Luke O'Farrell at full-forward, marked by yours truly.

It didn't go too well, however, for either Thurles or myself. Luke got three goals, which was bad enough, but his third came with the last puck of the game to win it. The ball came across, he caught it, turned, and bang – back of the net. That was end-of-the-world stuff, but somehow it got worse. Liam Sheedy was the Tipperary minor manager and he'd gone to the game to have a good look at the prospects coming through. Not a great day to have the player you were marking get a hat-trick, including the match-winner.

Midleton went on to win the competition. They had a good team, but we'd been confident going up against them in the semi. And I couldn't help thinking, *Is this ever going to happen?* Losing a Féile final, losing a Harty final (even if we weren't fancied), losing in the All-Ireland series and feeling we were miles off the standard, losing a Harty semi-final when we expected to win. At that point after losing a few games, I was thinking that maybe club was my level.

Sheedy picked the minor panel and I made it as a sub. I'd made the Tony Forrestal Tipperary team (under-14) with the likes of Séamus Hennessy, Brendan Maher and Mikey Cahill, and I made the Arrabawn team (under-16). But I wouldn't have stood out on those sides, in all honesty. Someone like Brendan Maher was standing out, he was one of the main lads, while I was just about making the team.

After that Harty semi-final defeat against Midleton we all went out in Thurles, even the couple of 17-year-olds like me, sneaking in to the pub. The following morning there was a Tipp minor trial, a game against Limerick up in

Newport that was the last trial before finalising the squad. It probably sounds a bit harsh, hauling a few lads who'd lost a Harty semi-final out to play minor for the county the following day, but with players of 17 or 18 years of age, management probably felt they didn't have to contend with hangovers. They didn't either, apart from one or two geniuses.

That time I wouldn't have had any interest in a drink but after the night out in Thurles one of the lads stayed in my house. We got back around 1 a.m. and didn't want the night to end, so I got out two eggcups and a bottle of whiskey and suggested a shot each as a nightcap.

We had a couple of shots and stayed up chatting until three, which wasn't ideal preparation for dragging myself out of bed at eight to catch a bus to Newport.

I was a sub, which was grand, but I got sent in for the second half, which wasn't. I ended up running over the ball. Missing it. Useless. Eventually I was shoved into full-forward just to keep me out of harm's way. On the way home from that game I thought it was all over for me before it had even begun. Liam and the lads knew we'd been out, and if they hadn't before, they were in no doubt once they saw how I performed.

That was a Sunday morning. The following Tuesday I was

walking down from the school for a maths grind and the phone rang: Martin Gleeson from Gortnahoe-Glengoole who was a minor selector with Liam Sheedy. *Shit, this is it,* I thought. Martin said they'd picked the panel and they were giving me a chance: 'The carry-on last weekend, you know that's not the way to go. Show us what you're made of.' I was 17 years old then. Years later, Liam Sheedy would often jokingly remind me of that time when he gave me the chance.

Back then, I knew I'd got a break, and I was determined to make the most of it.

Advanced placement: learning in a hurry

Underage teams are fine (by which I mean Tony Forrestal tournaments and so on) but at that time there were no development squads. We weren't being brought in a couple of times a week to Dr Morris Park (the training grounds in Thurles), say, with the aim of improving and developing us as players, with a competitive game as a county team at under-14 at the weekend. The system wasn't set up like that back then.

And because of that, minor was the focus. You realised soon enough the level of seriousness with which it was treated, something that filtered through to you as a kid, even. If you were walking around Thurles, one of the pals might nudge you and say, 'Look at your man over there, he's playing minor for Tipp,' and that made an impression.

My main asset that time wasn't so much physical strength as an ability to read the play. Even early on in my senior career there were teams like Kilkenny who'd play the ball long, so you could anticipate deliveries and take a chance, and that was definitely the case when I was playing minor. That comes from playing centrally all the way up with the school and the club. You get used to moving left, moving right. At times I played up front at underage, which gave me some appreciation of what a forward wants, but I was always a more natural back. It was easier facing the ball, anticipating where the opposing defence planned to deliver it.

I also got stronger as I got older, even without hitting the gym, which was a help. Training was very much focused on skills and laps and sprints, but weight training wasn't really an option at minor level. That strength and anticipation complemented being good in the air. I'm left-handed, which I believe is a help if you're on a right-hander – you come in around the opponent, if you like. I don't think it was an accident that J.J. Delaney played left hand on top, as well as T.J. Reid, Larry Corbett and John O'Brien, who were excellent hurlers. And something many of those left-handers had in common was an ability to arrive late under a dropping ball, drive across the players already there, and then win the ball. It can be hard for opponents to judge where players like that are coming from, but it stood to me. It might look awkward to spectators, but it definitely helped players.

I had a close connection as well with Paddy McCormack, my uncle, who was Tipperary minor manager until 2004, so I had a good idea of what went on at that age group. The likes of Paddy Stapleton, Kieran Bergin and Darragh Egan were on that team, as well as Shane Long, who went on to impress playing professional football. Tipp won a couple of Munster minor titles in Paddy's time. His first year as manager I remember tagging along to a tournament in Kildare (I was around 12, brought along for my skills as a water-boy again) and that made an impression on me, seeing these fellas representing the county. Serious players operating at a serious level.

So when I got the call-up to the minor squad in 2006, I knew it was the big show. Personally I would have felt

I was slightly off the level in some ways. I might have survived at Harty level but I was still only 16, and some lads were right on the age, the full 18 years. My realistic goal was getting a spot on the panel as opposed to making the first 15. Taking a step back and looking coldly at my Harty experience, I'd been solid, I'd done my job most of the time, but I hadn't been standing out in games, which I felt you had to do to make the county minor team.

Looking around the dressing room when the full minor panel was togging out, I'd have estimated there were seven or eight players who were more highly thought of than myself and more likely to make the team. That wasn't all bad, either. My thinking was, if I made the panel in 2006 then I'd surely be close to starting the following year, when I'd be on the age and have more experience.

On that team, Joey McLoughney from Toomevara was the captain and playing minor for the third year, so to me he was light years ahead. Brendan Maher was a key player, the likes of Timmy Dalton, John O'Keeffe and Séamus Hennessy were big names. To show the difference, Séamus Callanan was on that Tipperary minor selection, for instance, and the previous year, 2005, he had played in the county senior final for Drom and Inch against Thurles Sarsfields. We knew about him because we're in the same division, and at under-12, under-14 level and so on he was a player you had to watch, he was so good. Every time you played them, you had to make a plan to stop him.

In 2005 I played a county final as well, but at under-16 level. Séamus was playing in a county senior final against county players and seasoned men while I was playing against 15-year-olds, so I felt there was a huge gap between him and me. Pa Bourke, a relation of mine and a good friend, was involved with the Thurles Sarsfields senior team Séamus played against, so he was up at that standard as well. In time he was brought in by Babs Keating for the Tipp senior team at 18, so he was another player doing well at a very young age.

My aim was to get on the panel with those players and hope for a starting jersey in 2007. Liam Sheedy would have seen me up close for the whole of 2006 as well, which would help me the following season. Liam Sheedy was to be a significant part of my career, but at that stage I didn't know him that well. He was minor manager and I knew he had hurled for Tipperary but he hadn't had a long career. When I thought of the players of that era the likes of Tommy Dunne or Declan Ryan came to mind, they were the big names.

He had been the minor manager in 2005 as well, and I

knew of him because Pa Bourke was on that minor team and mentioned him the odd time. Liam had a good way about him, he could have a laugh with the players but you were always aware there was a line and you didn't go beyond that line. To be fair to him, in my memory he wasn't as strict as you might imagine with us as minors, though that might have been him reading the room and adjusting to a group of 17- and 18-year-olds, feeling he couldn't be too harsh with us.

To illustrate how differently things were done even then compared to now, Liam would have taken a lot of the training himself as well as being manager. That was different when he became the senior manager and he had to delegate work to the coaches, but when he was with the minors he was still only in his mid-thirties, so he wasn't long out of the playing scene himself. The sessions were very much skills- and drills-orientated, while the physical stuff would have been sprints and laps. Strength and conditioning was still a distance away for us.

I felt I was hanging on by my fingernails in training, in all honesty. The forwards I was up against were good and I was just trying to break even with them, and sure enough I didn't start the first couple of games in the Munster minor championship. I felt like the lad who'd be wearing number 24 or number 26. We beat Limerick in Thurles in the semi-final and I didn't even come on in that game. We were training on the Thursday night before the Munster minor final, which was to be played before the senior game, pucking the ball over and back across the field, and Liam was walking around, having a quiet word with the players as he went. Eventually he came to me.

'Well, how are you feeling?'

'Grand altogether.'

'You're getting the nod on Sunday. Enjoy it, you deserve it.'

Christ.

I went home and told the mother, and she said, 'Grand.' She wouldn't have made a big issue out of it. The next two or three nights ... you're shitting bricks, basically. I would have been on holidays from school and not that busy anyway, and maybe that didn't help. I ended up thinking and thinking about the game.

The Saturday night was an example of how not to prepare. I was struggling to sleep and ended up making a big deal out of it, looking at the clock and thinking, *If I get to sleep now I'll get seven good hours*. The fact that Tipp were playing Cork meant there'd be a big crowd there, the biggest by far I'd ever played in front of. That was in my mind. So was the player I'd be on, a chap called Patrick Horgan. 'Hoggie' was known to us back then. He was one of those players whose name drifts out of his own county and into other places. He was playing full-forward and I'd be picking him up.

It was Cork–Tipperary in the senior final as well. That had an impact because more of the crowd tends to come in for the minor game if the same two counties are playing in the senior. Naturally enough they have more of an interest in the curtain-raiser. I was nervous. Not only was it a Munster final, I hadn't played in any of the preceding games. And I hadn't played full-back that much either. When I started playing Harty with the school I was moved to full-back, and the county minor management were looking around for a full-back, but with the Sarsfields I usually played centre-back, centre-field or centre-forward.

Between making my debut, making my debut on Patrick Horgan in a Munster final, making my debut in Semple Stadium … there was plenty of material going around my head. The crowd was certainly a factor. In the previous game against Limerick the attendance was the players' families and a couple of diehards; you'd be lucky to have 2,000 people there. For the final Semple was full, with nearly 50,000 in attendance. And when you haven't had previous games to draw on, that builds up in your head, that the crowd will be unbelievable, that you can't make a mistake, that everyone will be staring at you. From that point of view, it was a great learning experience in terms of training myself about how to blot out the crowd. Instead of thinking, *I can't let this ball drop* or *If he gets another point they'll all be looking at me*, the game became the focus.

Cork beat us well enough, and Patrick was decent too, but I felt I grew into the game and settled. I was the new man in the full-back line and the thought that I'd be fired out to the sideline if I didn't do well didn't last. I got involved in the game and found I could live at that level. A couple of weeks later, we played Carlow in the All-Ireland quarter-final and we beat them well without shooting the lights out, and I was full-back again. Survived.

That got us a date in Croke Park against Kilkenny in the All-Ireland semi-final. Croke Park. I'd never played there before, which was intimidating enough, but Kilkenny had another decent full-forward for me: Richie Hogan. The last time I'd seen Richie was when playing with the school in the All-Ireland colleges. He and the St Kieran's lads beat us well, and at that stage I felt they were miles ahead of us. But with Tipperary it was different. We went well that day and won, making it to an All-Ireland final against Galway. That was a breakthrough for Tipperary. It was ten years since we'd won an All-Ireland minor title and the last senior All-Ireland had been in 2001, so there was a good buzz around the county.

Preparing for that 2006 minor All-Ireland was another learning process. By then I'd got into the habit of staying away from people for the couple of days before a big game if at all possible, keeping to my own company. I felt that people chatting to me in those few days might put a seed of doubt in my mind without meaning to, and I wanted to avoid that. So, the Friday and Saturday I'd be at home, strolling the roads, maybe pucking the ball off the wall. That made for a long two days, mind. The Saturday in particular would drag. Towards the end of my career I relaxed and wouldn't think twice about heading in to meet a pal for a coffee the day before a game. I'd be up early on the Saturday doing stretches, or maybe sharpening up the touch with 20 minutes in the ball alley. But that all comes with experience. Back then it was about checking what sport might be on the television on the Saturday, maybe a golf tournament that would put down the day for me.

More complications: I was driving from the age of 17 so I was sent to the shop on Saturday mornings to get the papers and a bottle of milk or whatever. That meant I'd be reading the papers, of course, even though a couple of years later, with the Tipp seniors, the paper was the last thing I'd be looking at. At that time, though, the morning before the All-Ireland minor final, I hauled myself out of the bed at around 10 and had a big bowl of corn flakes, or some other breakfast a nutritionist would ban nowadays. And then I went in and got the papers and was reading about Joe Canning this and Joe Canning that. Would he win his third All-Ireland medal if Galway got over Tipperary?

If there was a buzz about Patrick Horgan and Richie Hogan – and there was, deservedly so – that was nothing compared to the buzz about Galway's full-forward ahead of that All-Ireland final.

Joe was going for his third All-Ireland minor medal in a row. The whole country knew about it. Joe had already won an All-Ireland club medal at senior level, and not as number 26 on the panel either, but as the main danger man up front. There were rumours he might be tried by the Galway seniors before he left the minor grade. In Thurles we had a particular interest in the story because there was a local twist: Jimmy Doyle had been the last player to win three minor medals in a row, and he was a Sarsfields man.

And, of course, I'd be the one to mark Joe. It wasn't a time when teams came up with elaborate plans or sweepers to counteract opponents, but the selectors had made an excellent switch in the semi-final by moving Brendan Maher to corner-back, and they left him there for the final. Brendan was good enough to play in any line of the field, so that move gave us a bit more security in the full-back line. But when Joe came strolling in to full-forward at the start of the game it was just me and him on the edge of the square.

The team would meet up at the Midway in Laois, the traditional meeting spot, that Sunday. The Mid bus would have brought us there to join the main team bus to head to Croke Park. It was clear soon enough that this was a different level, and I don't just mean our route to Dublin. We went all the way along the hard shoulder, flying, a Garda escort from the Midway to the capital. The crowds were bigger, meeting in the hotel beforehand was different, the tension coming along the road to the stadium. Everything.

Back then I was quiet in the dressing room, certainly. A lot of us took a few minutes to puck around in the adjoining astroturf area, but as minors there aren't many players who are going to stand up and take over the room, giving a speech. Basically we were waiting for Liam Sheedy to call us in. Joey, as captain, said a few words, and then Liam spoke, having told us to form a circle in the middle of the room. He was very good, everything was positive and aimed at making you feel confident: 'No one is going to stop you today.' He revved us up and out we went. Croke Park on All-Ireland final day is full-on, though. Out into the noise and it's an experience. You have a moment where you think to yourself, *Christ. This is it, it's real. It's serious.*

In a funny way, because so much of the focus was on Joe and the third medal and all of that, there wasn't as much pressure on me, or at least I wasn't putting that much pressure on myself. Before the throw-in my thoughts would have been along the lines of *Feck it, I'll have a go here.* We were probably around the same height, but when he came into full-forward next to me I could see he was very strong; at that stage I was thin as a rake and a year under the age, so I was conscious he had an advantage over me in that department.

In the game I didn't puck a lot of ball but I got in a couple of blockdowns and kept the ball away from him. I certainly wasn't as nervous as I'd been in the Munster final. Pa Bourke got a goal early on and settled us and we were going well, and that obviously gave the rest of us confidence. People pointed out afterwards that Joe didn't score from play in the game, but he was clearly a class player. Late on we were well on top and I was praying that the referee would blow it up before Joe did something outrageous and score a couple of goals. When the final whistle went, I remember jumping into the crowd and meeting some of the lads from the club. I was delighted, obviously, but there was also a sense of, *What's happened?* About six months earlier I was hoping to make the panel, and after the incident with the eggcups that looked doubtful, yet here I was now, having marked Patrick Horgan, Richie Hogan and Joe Canning. With an All-Ireland medal to show for it.

I felt more confident after that campaign. I fell back in with the club and won minor counties in hurling and Gaelic football. I played Gaelic football until the age of 21, but my heart was always more in the hurling. I also felt like a more senior player within that group, a leader, even though I was still only 17. The same when I fell back in with the Tipperary minors the following year, 2007. I felt I was part of it. In 2006 I was hanging in there by my fingertips; in 2007 I could say to myself, *Well, I was able for an All-Ireland minor final, I'll be able for this.*

I'd been disappointed at underage and colleges levels, but it just goes to show how quickly things can turn around: between March and September 2006 everything had changed. I'd grown up a lot.

On top of all that I got a glimpse of the future. The

four of us – Pa Bourke, Michael Gleeson, Michael Cahill and myself – from Thurles Sarsfields on the county minor selection were called into the club senior team for the county championship. It wasn't the greatest year for the club but I got on for a couple of the games and that helped my confidence. It suggested I could survive at club level. Only the year before, when I was with the under-16s, I'd seen the Sarsfields senior team play in a county final; 12 months later I had an All-Ireland medal in my back pocket and was able to hold my own with those same lads. No one has to say it out loud and you don't even have to say it to yourself, but you're growing up and getting more mature, almost unknown to yourself, and you realise you have a chance of becoming part of the whole thing.

Elsewhere, the Leaving Cert was another part of growing up. I couldn't say I worked really hard at the books; I have to admit I found the books tough going. I got through and qualified for a course in Waterford Institute of Technology – construction economics – and I took up the place, but it was only for the sake of going. I started in WIT on the Thursday after the minor final. Not the greatest timing, to put it mildly. We had the homecoming to Thurles on the Monday, then up to Toomevara to Joey McLoughney's club, so that was Monday and Tuesday taken care of, and I had my debs dance on the Wednesday night. A right week.

My mother dropped me down to Waterford and the following day I texted Séamus Callanan, who was starting in WIT as well.

Are you going in?

I don't know, are you going in?

I don't feel like it.

We ended up in the WIT sports bar, the Dome, drinking cider and thinking college was great craic altogether. But once the novelty wore off I was gone. It was a course that didn't suit me and I wasn't six weeks in Waterford before coming back home.

My uncle Paddy was working in what was then Tipperary Institute, now TUS Thurles Campus, and he advised me to chat to an administrator there (it was still very early in the academic year) and I got onto a business studies course. It made more financial sense to live at home and attend college in Thurles, even though my interest in business studies was on a par with my interest in construction studies. After a couple of years I more or less stumbled into an apprenticeship in plumbing. That suited me better, so I went for it and packed in college.

Come 2007 I was on the Tipperary minor team again. There were new people at the helm: Declan Ryan was in as manager, Tommy Dunne was the coach, and Liam Cahill was a selector that year, three lads who would impact my career in different ways. Declan, an all-time great with Tipperary, was different to Liam Sheedy. He stood back and gave more freedom to Tommy with the coaching. He'd give the spiel after training or before a game to fire you up, but in general he was more laid-back.

Tommy was Tommy. He's never changed, that intensity was always there. Back then we would have known who he was, he was the main man on the Tipperary team that I and the rest of the minors had grown up watching. All the skills, a beautiful striker, we were all in awe of him before he ever came onto the field. He had us eating out of the palm of his hand when he started training us. Whatever he wanted us to do, we'd do it. Instantly. Tommy was great to drive you on. Even if you were doing well with a drill, he'd still drive you: 'Come on, there's more in you, there's more.' He was the same ten years later when he came in with the seniors – he still looked like he'd done a full session afterwards rather than just the coaching, he put so much of himself into it.

Back then it was all about the skills, and the speed of your skills. Everything had to be sharp, fast, faster – your hurling had to be top notch so he'd always drive you to quicken your striking: 'Quicker, quicker, quicker, you can do it quicker, you're able.' But he also had a good way about him when it came to encouraging players. It wasn't all shouting – you'd be wrecked after a good run of drills and he'd come up behind you and hit you in the back: 'That's the shot, well done, it's in you,' and the eyes bulging out of his head. If Tommy hits you a slap across the backside and tells you you're doing well, you grow ten feet tall. In one drill you might have run over the ball a couple of times or mishit a shot (and Tommy would let you know if you made a mistake) but his encouragement was a huge part of training. It made you grow as a player, no doubt about it, and it made you enjoy the session even more.

Liam was only starting off in management. He was good to talk to players but he wouldn't have had as big a role as Declan or Tommy at the time. The funny twist was that Liam was playing with Thurles Sarsfields that season, 2007. He had transferred in from Ballingarry so I had him as a selector with the Tipperary minors, and I had him as a team-mate with the club. Looking back, it was a bit surreal. I was starting matches with Sarsfields at centre-back, and Liam was a terrific forward, so we'd cross swords the odd time in training games. So, it was a case of Saturday morning, Dr Morris Park, being coached by Liam with the Tipp minors, and the following morning flaking him at club training (not too hard, though).

There was a difference with the Tipperary minors for me because I'd been there the previous year and won an All-Ireland. It wasn't a matter of making speeches in the dressing room to your fellow 18-year-olds about standards – that's not how minors operate, at least not back then – but I would have trained as hard and as well as I could, to show leadership. In general I'd consider myself a good trainer, I'd pour myself into every session, pushing myself as hard as I could. Unless you treat every training session with the level of seriousness you treat a game – correction: a big game with your club or county – then you won't improve.

It's something I'd like to be able to look back on and say that I gave every session everything I had. Later, when the gym became a bigger part of inter-county preparation I probably focused too much on gym work, even away from the group – I became addicted to it. Back then, in 2007, I was doing more than the scheduled sessions with Tipperary. I'd find a track for running sessions, or if I went for a swim in the Anner Hotel, pure recovery, I'd start thinking, *If I did a bit of a run on the treadmill for 20 or 30 minutes, it'd stand to me*, so I'd do that before the pool.

It probably stood to me in terms of discipline and commitment, even if today's sports scientists would balk at the training load I was putting on myself. Back then you could play a championship match with Tipperary and be released back to the club for a week. Going back to the Sarsfields my mindset would be, *I better show these lads that my fitness is at an inter-county level*, and I'd end up training like a lunatic. But it did stand to me, even if I overdid it at times. The mental strength it gives a player shouldn't be underestimated: before a big game you can say to yourself, *I've the work done and more, and I didn't cut any corners. This is going to show in the last quarter.*

In 2007 I was on the Tipp minor team but I was also on the Sarsfields minor hurling and football teams, on the Tipperary Institute team, on the Sarsfields under-21 and senior teams, and, for a couple of weeks, the Tipperary under-21 hurlers. Busy times, but you're 18 and full of energy, you feel you can keep going forever. Myself and Brendan Maher were only pulled in for a few sessions with the under-21s, but it was still something else to fit into the calendar.

On the minor team there were a few faces who'd become very familiar. Noel McGrath had figured in 2006 but he was only 16 then; the next year he was more involved and he was a starter. (He was well on the road by then, though. His club, Loughmore-Castleiney, won the Munster senior club championship that year and he was one of their key players.)

Seamus Hennessy was there in 2006 as well, while Bonner Maher was another lad who made an impression, mostly for the big head of hair he had then! His approach was always the same: win the ball and tear through, bouncing off opponents. We had a good core of lads involved over those couple of years, and a huge number of them came through to the Tipperary senior team. Myself, Brendan Maher, Bonner, Noel, Séamus Callanan, Michael Cahill – not to mention the likes of Pa Bourke, Séamus Hennessy, John O'Keeffe, Tom Stapleton, Gearoid Ryan, who also played senior for the county.

If you look at any senior club team in Ireland, it's rare that they'll get more than one or two per year from the minor team. For the Tipperary seniors to get that number from a couple of minor teams was very unusual, though the players I've mentioned were also very dedicated, and level-headed enough to keep at it. And the management was key too: Liam Sheedy and his selectors were good with us, and the following year Declan, Tommy, Liam Cahill and Michael Gleeson senior, the other selector, didn't let us get carried away either. They stressed that there was an importance to every year even if a few of us had All-Ireland medals won. That was crucial. There wasn't any danger of us losing our way – if anything, I trained harder in 2007 than I had the previous season.

We got through Munster handily enough, beating Cork in the final. The fact that it was in Thurles was a help – looking back now, a lot of our big games at underage level were in Thurles, which didn't hurt at all, playing in front of home support on a ground we knew better than the opposition.

That Munster final was a huge boost – both in terms of the occasion and the opposition. I knew there'd be a big roar for Cork when they came out, but that it would die down after a few seconds and settle before the game started. And the experience of coming up against some big names the previous year also made a difference. I could say to myself that I'd marked Patrick Horgan, Richie Hogan and Joe Canning, and that – with all due respect to our opponents in 2007 – it was unlikely I'd meet players quite as good as those three.

In addition, my own game had improved over the previous 12 months. That was evident in my match-up with Luke O'Farrell in the Munster final of 2007 and that year's All-Ireland final a few months later. Luke had taken me for three goals in the Harty Cup in 2006, and I'd been very nervous having to mark him while playing for Tipperary. And although in 2007 I had the usual nerves before a big game, I was boosted by the experience I'd gained in winning an All-Ireland minor medal and playing senior for Sarsfields. I settled into games quicker and got to the pitch of them faster.

Another minor All-Ireland title followed in 2007 and confidence was definitely starting to rise.

A Sunday in September: making an All-Ireland senior hurling final

Coming onto the club senior team, the company was good. Liam Cahill, Eddie Enright, Larry Corbett, 'Redser' O'Grady, who was Tipperary captain the year before, Johnny Enright, who'll go down as one of the greatest club hurlers in Tipperary – that was the quality we had. I was playing centre-back, sometimes full-back, so I felt I was doing something right. Building on the performances with the Tipp minors. Progressing.

Working late one November night in 2008, a dark, miserable evening, I got a phone call. It was Liam Sheedy, asking if I would come in to the Tipperary senior panel. Would I what?! It wasn't a shock. Liam had put together a good panel and had won the Munster title in 2008 (Davy Fitzgerald's Waterford had beaten them in the All-Ireland semi-final) but he was obviously looking to freshen things up, and the minors of 2006 and 2007 were going to come into the picture.

Sarsfields had reached the county final in 2008, and although we lost, I knew I was going well in those games. If the selectors were going to the matches, they were bound to notice me, I felt. We'd lost the All-Ireland under-21 final in 2008 to a good Kilkenny side – T.J. Reid, Paul Murphy, Richie Hogan – but I got the man-of-the-match award, which was some consolation.

(A mad one before that final when we did our pre-game warm up in a club pitch in Dublin. Declan Carr was the manager, a former Tipperary All-Ireland winning captain. Declan was a tough trainer, big into his fitness and strength, big into hard work, basically. We did our warm-up, then he had us down on the ground for sit-ups. We must have done 150 sit ups and just as we thought we were finished, he said, 'Now we'll do 50 press-ups for Kilkenny,' so we did 50 press ups. Then he said, 'We'll do 50 for the people of

Tipperary', and we did those. Stomach and arms hanging with lactic acid about 60 mins before an All-Ireland final. Times have changed, thankfully.)

All things considered, I felt I was in the shop window, and it probably helped that Liam knew us all from the minors, but still, when you get the call for the county senior team it's a big moment. You know the hard work is just beginning, but you also know how much hard work has got you to that point.

The whole thing accelerated quickly, looking back. In March 2006 I was getting cleaned out in a Harty Cup game, the following September I had an All-Ireland minor medal and club county minor medals, and by November 2008 I was called into the Tipperary senior team. I got bigger and stronger but my confidence was growing too. I was coming up against the best of players and holding my own at least.

There was some business to take care of first, though. We were in the county under-21 hurling final that year, on 21 December 2008 in Templemore. I can remember being on the field and seeing spectators coming into the venue dressed as Santa Claus. On the 23 December, we went for DEXA scans, which evaluate muscle mass and body fat and so on, for the Tipperary seniors. (Managers like to get those tests done before the training starts, because it becomes obvious fairly quickly who is or isn't going to the gym, or sticking to the nutrition plan, when the next round of scans are done.)

Myself and Pa Bourke went down together that morning for the scans. We'd won the under-21 final two days beforehand, so it was just as well the DEXA wasn't looking for beer in the system, and my muscle mass would have been very low, looking back now. I didn't have much gym work done, if any, though my body fat was fine. My wrist was sore as I'd got a slap in that under-21 final but it hadn't stop me playing – or celebrating – and Christmas was only a day or two away. More celebrating before hitting Dr Morris Park for training after New Year's Eve.

That first night back training with Tipperary, my wrist was still sore. The running was no bother but when we had to get down for press-ups I couldn't put any pressure on.

Sheedy was walking past: 'What's wrong?"

'I can't go down,' I said.

He sent me off with Dr Peter Murchan to Clonmel for an X-ray. Broken wrist. Some start to the senior career.

The bone was snapped, so it was a cast. No hurling for six to eight weeks. Sheedy and the management were good; there was plenty of other work I could do apart from hurling, so I kept going to training. Cian O'Neill, the strength and conditioning coach, had me doing runs and bike work, and I was never as fit. I was naturally big and getting stronger.

Before then I had done some gym work, but in a very unstructured way, the odd bit of weights here and there. But even that stood to me and meant I was better conditioned than I might otherwise have been, and better suited to surviving at senior inter-county level. But with a broken wrist I wasn't doing any of that. It was running and cycling. And no hurling, obviously, which to me meant I was going to be dropped. How could the management carry a player in his first year who couldn't even come on as a sub?

In fairness, though, back then they'd name 26 for a league game and bring five or six more members of the panel in tracksuits along as well. So, I was in my tracksuit at those first few games as a spectator. From that vantage point, inter-county looked like a huge step up, but as the wrist recovered and I could play in games in training, I felt I was able to stay afloat. I wasn't that far off, even if the quality was very good.

It helped that there were familiar faces with me. Bonner Maher, Mickey Cahill, Brendan Maher, Noel McGrath, Séamus Hennessy, Gearoid Ryan – they were all brought in with me, and Séamus Callanan and Pa Bourke were already there. When we went for the DEXA scans I was sitting in a room with half a dozen lads I knew well – all familiar faces. I knew nearly ten lads already rather than having to get to know strangers who were years older than me, lads I only knew from watching as a supporter. Because so many of the minors I played with were there, I was able to say to myself, *They're the same as me.* That all helped. So did the fact that I was heading to training with Larry Corbett and Pa, Mickey Cahill – lads I knew well from the club.

There were leaders in that dressing room. Eoin Kelly, Brendan Cummins, Declan Fanning, Paul Curran Conor O'Mahony. That was a lot of experience, and the atmosphere was good. Liam Sheedy was the manager and he had great people with him: Mick Ryan and Eamon O'Shea were selectors and Cian O'Neill was doing the strength and conditioning. They all contributed to a good atmosphere, and the players had won the Munster title under Liam the previous year, so they were optimistic and that helped create a feel-good factor.

Eoin Kelly was a big presence in the dressing room. A great talker, whether it was telling lads what was needed or revving them up before a big game. He had that aura about him because of what he had done on the field over the previous years. Willie Ryan from Toomevara was the official captain that year but he was a sub, so Eoin was the on-field captain. And when he spoke everyone listened. The respect was total.

But at the same time, when you were training you could have the craic with him as well. No matter if you were

19 and in your first year on the team or if you were five years older than him, Eoin had a way of getting along with everyone. Great man for the one-liners too, even if some of them wouldn't be suitable for print.

But when it was serious and Eoin Kelly spoke to the team before a championship game, say, then everyone sat up and paid attention, and clicked into championship mode. Sheedy was cute in the way he would use Eoin to give a speech to the players, the way he picked his moments to unleash Eoin to deliver a speech that would have us frothing at the mouth.

Eoin, his brother Paul, Micheál Webster, Larry, Shane McGrath, Conor O'Brien — they were all great lads to poke fun at you, and no better targets than the crowd of greenhorns who'd landed in. The same lads would often get tangled up poking fun at each other too, which could get messy, but anyone who knows how teams operate knows that that kind of slagging is how players make newcomers feel part of the group.

I think it helped that we, the younger players, applied ourselves from the off. The older players might have wondered beforehand whether we'd fit in, but I think they saw soon enough that we were serious about what we were doing, that we did the gym work, did the field work, prepared properly. It all worked well: the experienced lads accepted the new lads, the new lads worked hard, and Liam was the ideal man at the top of the tree, keeping it all moving and creating a good environment.

Eamon O'Shea was a big part of that, and even though I didn't know who he was then, he would become a huge influence on my career. He hadn't been involved with Liam before and his own playing career went back to the early 1980s and a very successful club career with a great club, Kilruane McDonaghs. At the first training sessions I was thinking, *Is this lad half-mad?* He'd bring up something that had happened in the last match we'd played, and then he'd head off, running on to chat to other players. He never overburdened us with information. Sometimes the message at training might be as simple as, 'You're doing well, outstandingly well,' before moving on to another player, but he was always giving you energy, giving you confidence, a real player's man.

For instance, he might tell the group to improve but individually he wouldn't put a player down. In one-on-ones he was very good, in the same way as Liam. If you felt down in the dumps or felt you'd had a tough day in the last game, then a five-minute chat with Eamon had you feeling a million dollars and only bursting for the next match. There was no such thing as loads of cones and bollards on the field when he was training us, it was all coming from his head: 'You there, you there and you there,' and then, 'Now lads, ye work it out.' At times it could be tiring to keep up with him before a ball was even pucked.

That approach was different for me. I would have been accustomed, at minor training sessions, to going out to cones and drills and a session planned out beforehand. Now, he probably had it planned out in his head but to us it looked chaotic until he got going and made sense of it. He was into freedom and playing with the shackles off (diagonal movement was very important) but one of his major points to us always was that the game itself is unstructured. Anything can happen in a game, he'd say, but one thing that doesn't happen is running to one cone and turning with the ball to go to another cone. So a lot of his training was based on that idea (or avoiding that cone-based idea, put it that way) but it was fantastic. He changed forward play in Tipperary with his emphasis on movement, and if there was a split in training he'd go with the forwards to one end of the field. We'd be with Liam and Mick Ryan, the backs, at the other end.

But there was a benefit to us as well because as defenders we had to deal with the forwards Eamon was coaching: they brought a different approach in mixed matches and training sessions, so that sharpened us as backs too. There were other differences, though. Eamon had the lads looking for flicks and touches, creating space, vision, but Mick and Liam were more about digging in and not giving an inch to your forwards. Coaching us in their own image, if you like – attacking the ball and getting to the ball first to dictate the play, clearing whatever was in front of you out of the way. Overall, that was a good balance. Eamon would be on to us as defenders to clear the ball to where the forwards wanted it – 'Push the ball in that direction' was his expression – while Mick and Liam instilled a more traditional attitude into the defence: stand up to it, don't back down.

It's not just a different level of coaching at inter-county; the physical demands of training are a step up as well. There were always tests, like the bleep tests, which let you know how tough it was. I was up near the top of the squad in the bleep tests, partly because I was always tipping along with an extra bit of training when I could manage it. It wasn't always appealing, and sometimes I thought I might be doing too much, but another good bleep test result was evidence enough that it was standing to me. They're not always regarded as the most scientific, but as a basic test of your appetite, the bleep test is hard to beat. I don't believe that fitness came naturally to me, I felt the evidence was in the hard work and effort (and sometimes overtraining) that stood to me throughout my career.

Bonner Maher was well ahead of the posse, his fitness level was insane. He just won all the bleep tests, simple as that. But because he was so fit, if you were second or third to him it was evidence enough that you were in good nick. It's not always scientific either. Lads like Conor O'Mahony, or Dan McCormack later on, didn't enjoy the bleep tests, but put them into a game and they covered the ground no bother. Ranged all over the field when there was a ball there to be won, and there was no end to them.

Eoin Kelly would have suffered in those bleep tests. Larry Corbett wouldn't have killed himself with them. But they were two lads you couldn't be without, obviously. Then there were lads who changed over the course of their careers, like Séamus Callanan. The difference between him starting out and now, in terms of fitness, strength, body shape, is huge: he was one of those lads who got stronger and stronger, fitter and fitter, as the years went on. Obviously one size doesn't fit all. I felt I needed that level of fitness for my confidence, to know I could compete with anyone. The likes of Eoin and Larry, once they were experienced, knew the level of fitness they needed in order to compete. Those levels aren't all the same, and they don't need to be.

When my wrist recovered I was promoted to the bench. I was there, for instance, when Tipp played Kilkenny in the 2009 league game in Nowlan Park, when Kilkenny made bits of us. That was a tough afternoon. We were sitting up in the stand with Kilkenny supporters all around us, and they weren't holding back, roaring down from the stand: 'The bus is running outside, lads.' That always stayed with me.

The last game of the league was against Galway above in Salthill, and I was named as a sub. We had to win it to stay in contention in the league. We were flying out to Spain to a training camp the day after which didn't exactly increase the pressure, but you certainly didn't want to be trooping onto a plane to go training having lost a big game the day before.

When we got to Salthill, Sheedy called me into a small room in the hotel before the pre-match meal: 'You're playing number six, Conor O'Mahony is sick.'

'Oh right,' I said, though I was thinking, *Christ, this changes things a bit.*

But I had so little time to think about it, it worked out perfectly. I didn't have time to get nervous or to overanalyse what I was going to do. I played well, and I think that game in particular convinced the selectors that I had something to offer the team right there and then, that I was ready.

I got sent a headline from a newspaper article the following morning from an ex-Tipperary hurler who said that my performance reminded them of the Tony Wall performances back in the day. He was a fellow clubman and Tipp great. 'Don't be getting carried away,' I replied.

We won the game 1–17 to 1–15 so the mood was great going to Spain. We'd got through to the knock-out stages, confidence was high after a close win away from home, and the morning after we landed it was straight into three training sessions a day. It's fantastic to be able to prepare like a professional even if it's only for a week, but it's hard work. There's a hurling session in the morning, gym session in the afternoon, hurling or running session in the evening. Constant.

You're getting a huge amount of training into your system, so there's a physical benefit. There's a mental benefit as well, the comfort of knowing you can take it. On the Wednesday evening we had a running session, soloing up and down the field in searing heat, wondering if the session was ever going to end, hanging in there ... that makes you stronger mentally. Waking up on the Thursday morning your first thought is, *How am I going to get through this today?* as you peel yourself out of the bed. But you get warmed up and you get through it. It gives you great confidence – you're getting through 15 or 16 training sessions in a few days.

And then you have the night out at the end as well. After beating Galway on the Sunday afternoon we stayed in a hotel in Dublin ahead of the flight the next day. Liam allowed us to have a beer or two that night, which meant we were a little bit tired heading out to Spain. Train hard all week, and the night before coming home you're allowed out as well. Couple of drinks. So heading home we also felt a bit seedy, but we learned from that. On future trips we socialised the first night we got to Spain; at least then we felt a million dollars on the way back.

There was one more league game to play, against Limerick in Thurles, and I was picked at wing-back. I had a doubt or two after that selection – I'd played a right match against Galway at centre-back, but now they were moving me? We got through that game and were in a league final against Kilkenny, and though Conor O'Mahony was still out of action, I didn't know what to expect in terms of the team the selectors would pick.

The Tuesday evening beforehand we were in Dr Morris Park, pucking in lines, back and forth, and Liam sidled up to me.

'You're playing six this Sunday. We'll be naming you at five but you're playing at six.'

Centre-back in a national final. Against Kilkenny. In my home pitch. Okay.

At that stage they'd won three in a row and the talk about that Kilkenny team was growing. As a kid I didn't think of Kilkenny as huge rivals to Tipperary, I saw the rivalry as more Munster-orientated, mainly because Tipperary weren't going hectic at the time.

But this Kilkenny side was getting that aura about it. The game in Nowlan Park earlier in the league now became a factor for us. We'd been hammered by them down there and the comments from the crowd about the bus waiting outside were still pretty fresh in my memory, so we were building the game up in our minds as a significant one.

Because that year was the 125th anniversary of the GAA, a lot of the finals were played in Thurles, and that was another factor, being at home. The cliché is that teams want to put down a marker in certain games, but the reality is that teams want to put down a marker in every game, and that was certainly a significant game for us. For long portions of the game, everything went so well. At one stage we were eight points up, which was surreal. James Woodlock and John O'Brien got goals and we were flying. At the other end of the field it was good news as well – Brendan Cummins made an unbelievable save from Henry Shefflin, who had got away from his marker. Not for the first time, either.

I learned a good bit myself that day because I was Henry's marker for most of it. I wouldn't have been unduly nervous marking him – he was an outstanding forward, obviously, an all-time great, but I felt confident ahead of the throw-in. In the game, his movement was very good, though. He had two points scored before I had even settled down. I won the next ball, and started winning frees, gaining confidence, but it was a ding-dong struggle. He was very cute in reading the game, always. He would take a chance on you missing the odd one or someone breaking the ball on to him. Then he'd be gone.

The way Kilkenny played suited me, because their approach was very different to the way teams play now. There was no passing the ball through the lines in 20-, 30-yard passes; if Tommy Walsh got the ball in his hand I'd be gone straightaway and leave Shefflin, because you could tell immediately where the ball was going to land. As time went on they got cute. They'd pop a short pass to someone in the middle of the field, or your own man would go short and collect a pass. But at that stage you could be gone before the ball was even struck.

Many people will remember Jackie Tyrrell burying Séamus Callanan with a shoulder; you'd probably be sent off for it now, but I had no issue with it. I'd have done the same myself if the situation was reversed. To be fair to Kilkenny, they showed their experience. Richie Hogan and Aidan Fogarty got goals and they hung in there to make a draw of it. In extra time they showed the cuteness and got the win, 4–17 to 2–26.

It was probably one of the greatest hurling matches to have been played, in my opinion. It ws certainly up there with the best of our all-Ireland battles with Kilkenny. I was taken off with cramp towards the end of extra time, absolutely gassed. Welcome to the big time!

We were disgusted afterwards, obviously, but in time we saw the benefits of that game. We'd done well and a lot of the newer lads had played – myself, Noel, Brendan came on, Séamus. There was a nice element of newness and the experience brought us on. We would bring that confidence into the championship.

The league final was ideal preparation for the Munster championship because it had been a championship game itself in all but name. How could you better prepare than with a game against the All-Ireland champions going to extra time? That said, the first-round game against Cork was another level altogether. The stadium was full, I knew I'd be picking up Ben O'Connor, another hurling hero, it was the Munster championship … the league is one thing, but the Munster championship is what we were all reared on. The ultimate competition. They had a different style, too; that Newtownshandrum running style was noticeable, even if it wasn't as pronounced as you'd see nowadays. But the experience we'd gathered in the league final stood to us; Séamus Callanan got the goal that made the difference and won the game.

I learned a lot in a hurry that year, particularly about preparation for big games. A few of the lads I'd hurled with at underage level were on the selection but weren't starting. Brendan Maher and Mickey Cahill were subs, for instance. Meanwhile I was puzzling out how to prepare myself for the big days. I still cut myself off on the Friday and Saturday before a game. Fridays weren't too bad but I hated Saturdays, particularly the night time and trying to sleep. At least on the Sunday I could get up and go for a walk to clear the head (I'd given up going for the papers by that point; the mother had to get them instead). Having the time to myself was a big plus on those mornings.

Later, after my grandparents Josie and Cissie had passed on, and my cousin Caroline, I made a habit of visiting them in the graveyards on the morning of games. I just found it very relaxing to have time to myself in the company of family.

Back then, we'd meet four hours before a game – if it was on in Thurles we'd head across to Horse and Jockey around 12, have a pre-match meal and hang around for a while. At least the group was together, though, and the stadium wasn't far away. Afterwards, we'd head to Littleton, where Cian O'Neill would have us warm up, and from there we'd get back on the bus and head into Thurles, so by the time the game rolled around we'd have to do another warm-up.

I went through phases with earphones – sometimes wearing them for music before a game, sometimes not – but the music on the bus was a big deal. When we'd get to within a minute of the stadium the key song for that year would be put on, something to get everyone bouncing. One year it was Johnny Cash. Coming up through the Square in Thurles – thronged with people wearing the colours of both counties – the music would drive the atmosphere on the bus, and then Johnny would start blasting out over the speakers to let you know: it was game time and to stay resilient. A great message.

We won the Munster semi-final against Clare in Limerick with something to spare and then it was Waterford in the final. First senior Munster final, but we had a bit of luck. Because it was the 125th anniversary, the match was on in Thurles. We had a lot of younger players breaking through, and because most of the significant games that year were on in Semple Stadium, it had to be a help to us.

We struggled at the start against Waterford, however, and after a while I was shifted in from wing-back to full-back. Dan Shanahan came in on top of me, and after what he had done in previous years, the goals he'd scored, I was feeling under pressure. But it went well for me – I hurled a right match and stayed at full-back for the rest of the year, basically.

There's a world of difference between wing-back and full-back. When I was coming on the scene and especially in my first few years playing senior with the club, playing full-back, management were saying their plan was to put me out centre-back to have more of an influence on the game. A centre-back or wing-back can have more of an impact because he's in a part of the field where the ball is in play more often. You can have big defensive moments in games as a half-back, but the way the game has gone, even a defender can have big *offensive* moments, laying on scores and getting scores himself.

The full-back's job is to mind the house. Chances are, you'll be the last line of defence, and it's about shutting down one of the opposition's main players. The days of winning a big ball dropped into the square, bursting out and sending it 100 yards back down the field, driving the crowd mad – they're well gone. It's a lot easier to play that way but the game has changed. People involved in hurling understand that for the full-back now it's about winning breaks, turning the ball over, giving a ten-yard pass to a team-mate.

The centre-back's job has changed too. Rather than the old number six dominating and hurling everything before him, it's now about organising and anchoring the defence as well, driving the team on. Limerick's Declan Hannon does that well. He picks his moments to go up the field and pick off a point or two, which catches the eye, but he's usually sitting back to mind the house. That's what makes a centre-back's job so hard, and for that to work out everyone on the team has to be working to help the centre-back, dropping back to support and cover him.

The centre-back needs to be physically strong, too. Every team is running the ball, and where are they going to run it only right down the middle? So, the number six has to be able to come out and meet those players, but if you look around, the defenders on all inter-county teams are all six foot tall and powerful men. Everyone is conditioned for what they need to face, particularly the successful teams. All of them have plenty of physical power.

Luckily enough I had Brendan Cummins behind me, who wasn't shy about talking and steering you through a game: 'Don't go too far, Paudie, watch left, watch left.' Even with 50,000 people in the ground you'd still hear him. Paul Curran was shifted into the corner then, which was even better. More experience to lean on. And the game itself was different anyway at that stage. You really only worried about your own man as opposed to being in a two-man full-back line with huge space to cover. The ball was bombed in on top of the pair of you more often than not: fight for it and may the best man win. My confidence was high because I was young and happy to have a go. I didn't see any pitfalls and I hurled away accordingly. Your outlook can change as you get older and more cautious, but at that stage I was hurling freely.

At the end of the Waterford game we had four points to spare. Munster champions. Twenty years of age. In Semple Stadium, in Thurles. What more could you want?

The routine after a game like that stayed pretty constant. Into the dressing room and get changed. Then stroll down into Thurles, to the Park Avenue restaurant for the post-match meal. The crowd would stay around and you'd mix with the supporters, having a couple of drinks. The older lads went out on the Monday but there was a share of us still involved with the under-21s so we had to knuckle down for a midweek game against Waterford. (Which didn't go too well: we were fancied, we had a strong team, but they beat us easily down in Dungarvan. Maurice Shanahan and Noel Connors were on that Waterford team. I was sick the day of the game, felt absolutely terrible. Dr Peter Murchan, the team doctor, put me to bed in the hotel for an hour's sleep beforehand – if he hadn't come up to wake me I'd still be there, I was so weak.)

By then the buzz was well and truly back in Tipperary. You could feel the change: people meeting you in the street and wishing you well. The first time I'd signed an autograph was after the minor homecoming in 2006 – the minor teams always go to the Cathedral in Thurles with the cup, and a child asked me for my autograph there. In 2009 there was more of that, but there was also a sense of *Do you really want my signature?* I'd be half-embarrassed signing something. I couldn't help but think, *Hey, I'm only just in the door here.*

Being full-back rather than wing-back didn't bother me. I was just starting out so the old cliché about being happy just to have a jersey was still true. I'd done well enough in the Munster final at full-back, and I felt confident enough. The following May after a game against Cork I was thinking more along the lines of *Get me out of here and out the field to the half-back line*, but in 2009 I was happy out. Ready for road.

The All-Ireland semi-final was one-way traffic. We beat Limerick by about 20 points – Larry got a hat-trick – but they weren't at the races at all. I presume there were issues behind the scenes but we could only play what was in front of us. (I heard since that John Kiely decided that day in Croke Park that he'd do something about Limerick and he got involved with the hurlers as a result of that game. Given what he's done since then, maybe we should have taken it a bit easier on them.)

Again, though, that fed into our narrative, that there was something special building in Tipperary. That we were on the way, and we had an All-Ireland final to look forward to. Looking back, I dealt with the build-up pretty well, all things considered. There was plenty of commentary about Kilkenny because they were looking for a fourth title in a row, so that took a bit of the focus off us. We had to organise suits, for instance, while also doing the preparation for the day.

Liam would have us lined up in Semple Stadium as though we were meeting the president, and then he'd get the public address switched on, blaring crowd noise and team announcements out to replicate the experience. We'd shake hands with 'Hotpoint', the kit man, who was standing in for the president. In retrospect it was funny, but it also served a purpose. If you do that, it's not so strange when you do it on the day of the final. And it showed Liam's attention to detail: some people might wonder what that means in practice, but that's a good example of it.

It's not that there were no nerves at all (being young

and carefree only extends so far). I remember the mother wanted to watch *Up for the Match* the night before the All-Ireland, so I had to put the foot down and send her out to the kitchen (the only time I ever got my way with the remote, I'd say). A bit unfair, maybe, particularly as she was the one looking after the All-Ireland tickets for me, but she understood.

In general we were in a good place. The confidence was high within the group, and for me there was great support from the other Thurles lads, Larry Corbett in particular. He's such a laid-back fella that it would relax you anyway to be in his company before a match, but he also had a way of boosting you: 'You were flying in training this evening,' he'd say, taking the heat off you. The compliments meant all the more because he was flying himself, he was in red-hot form.

For all that, when Johnny Cash came on in the bus that Sunday it hit home fairly fast. This is real. This is happening, right now. An All-Ireland is different. There's no doubt about that. Running out the tunnel, there were two lines of kids visible, there was a huge blue and gold ball and a huge black and amber ball, then we stepped onto the field, and the roar … When I say the stadium was shaking, I mean it. There's a sense of things blurring, almost, in your vision because the noise is so loud it disorientates you.

During the warm-up, Cian O'Neill was blowing a whistle and pointing, because nobody could make out a word he was saying; for every other warm-up all year you could hear him, but he had to point at the stations to send us around that day because of the noise.

I was at full-back and Richie Power was named at full-forward for Kilkenny, but Henry Shefflin jogged in at the start. Shit. Looking back it was a good move by Brian Cody. He probably said to Henry, 'This lad did well in the league final but he's the youngest on the Tipp team, the most inexperienced; go in there and rattle him.' In the first couple of minutes it nearly worked out, too – I went for a ball but it squirted under my feet and in to Henry. He pulled but Brendan got a nice touch on it and put it around the post. If that had gone in, the day could have gone differently. My whole career could have gone differently.

Benny Dunne was sent off for us in the second half, but for most people the Kilkenny goals are what stick in the mind, the first one in particular. Richie Power got the ball and drove towards goal. We all felt he'd overcarried and charged, and when the referee gave a penalty we couldn't believe it. Myself, Conor O'Mahony and Brendan were on the line but the ball flew in over my head. It was a good strike but for a long time I felt, *I should have got to that.*

Brendan pucked out and they came back. I went to the corner to get the ball but lost my hurley. Eoin Larkin passed into Martin Comerford: goal. The whole thing had got away from us. And that was a lesson – not to let a game get away like that. I genuinely felt before the match that we wouldn't be beaten. Shane McGrath got a point at one stage from well out the field and the crowd went bananas, and I was thinking, *Here we go now, this is a sign*. After that, a ball came down between myself and Richie Power and I won it. I came out, fielded it and blasted it back down the field (no placing the passes into someone's hand then). The roar from the crowd nearly lifted me physically, the shot of adrenaline was unbelievable.

We had chances. Séamus Callanan hit a shot that P.J. Ryan just got a touch to, when a goal would have swung it; Eoin Kelly nearly had another goal but lost his footing just at the wrong time. Two goals, though, and it's gone. It's almost worse when it's so close, when you think you'll win it. At the final whistle I hit the ground. Bawling. It felt like the world was going to end. In fairness to Brian Cody, he came over and shook hands – he wouldn't smile if they won, he wouldn't rub it in. In fairness that's the man he always was, in victory or defeat: he shook hands. Fair play, the best team won, now move on.

That was the famous year of plan B and keeping spectators

off the field, but the Kilkenny supporters came on anyway; they'd just won four in a row, you couldn't blame them. I remember turning around and seeing Tommy Walsh being carried off the field. After the cup was presented, we walked off into our dressing room. Benny Dunne was in an awful way after being put off, he obviously felt a responsibility about that. The rest of us were inconsolable as well. I remember Brian Cody coming in to say a few words, but after he left, Declan Fanning spoke. He said that Benny was our team-mate and we had to back him, that looking after each other had got us this close to an All-Ireland and we were going to continue to do that.

It was a great speech. He really hit the right note, and afterwards, even though I was heartbroken, I also felt proud. Proud of what we'd done. Proud of my team-mates.

The long road to the promised land

After the All-Ireland final defeat, we were back to our clubs. Not immediately after, not the next week, so we had that bit of time to ease back into it. We had a 'relaxing' few days touring around Tipperary after the final and blew off steam, as they say, before we got back to club action. We had a good run with the club when we got back, which took the focus off the disappointment of the All-Ireland, particularly when we won the county.

That was a big step. We'd gone 31 years without winning a county senior title, and when we won it in 2005 people were probably thinking, *That's it now, they're back*. But we went from 2006 to 2008 without another title, and that led to doubts. A few of us were brought through to the senior team, but we lost the divisional final in 2009 and had to take the back-door route from then on.

Winning that county title meant a lot – to me, to the club, to the area. We had a good age profile on the team, which augured well for the future. People sometimes harp on about the inter-county scene overshadowing the club, but for us that time the county title was a dream come true. Not that the entire experience was positive – we were winning well in the last couple of minutes against Drom and Inch in the 2009 county final, running down the clock, when I went for a ball with James Woodlock, my Tipperary team-mate. The two of us clashed for the ball and I heard a loud snap – I looked down expecting to see my hurley broken, but it wasn't. I turned, and James was in agony on the ground, his leg twisted the wrong way. Winning that county final meant a huge amount, and I won the man of the match award, but you never want to see someone suffer an injury like that, team-mate or opponent, let alone someone I was friendly with from the county side.

I mined a couple more positives out of 2009. I won an All-Star and we added the county under-21 title, so it was a pretty big year. At the start of the league I was just another player on the panel and then the whole thing took off.

In fairness to the county board, they brought us out to Los Angeles and San Diego, a great trip. That was my first time away with the Tipp senior team. Before that there was the All-Star trip to Buenos Aires. So, it wasn't real life at all, really, and I was happy to face into the new year and some form of normality again.

After 2009 I was confident. I'd learned a lot and been through a lot in one year, so I was looking forward to 2010. From the very start Liam and the rest of the backroom team made it clear that we'd be upping things a level or two, when it came to the intensity of training, for instance. And training did get harder, but to be fair to management they were right there with us. In Dr Morris Park it seemed like Liam or Cian O'Neill were practically doing the runs alongside us. No matter how bad the weather, they were there driving us along.

One particular evening, just after the team holiday, we were above in Dr Morris Park and the weather was absolutely terrible. Rain, hail, sleet lashing down, a savage wind, and everyone swaddled in rain gear, heavy pants, heavy top, running long sprints, soloing the ball, up and down the field. It tests you mentally, a night like that. You have to go, and go again, and it's desperate when you're ploughing up and down the field. But then you come into the dressing room and have a hot shower, and you start thinking, *You know, that wasn't the worst.* Those are the little steps, the small improvements.

Our physio Mick Clohessy was great to take the odd photograph on a night like that, unbeknownst to us, and then he'd pull out the pictures facing into a big championship game later in the year, just to show us the work we'd put in to get there. A brilliant idea.

We knew ourselves from the previous year that we were close to winning an All-Ireland, close to Kilkenny, and management knew too. And that was their way of squeezing that extra little bit out of us, and our way of accepting that we needed to give that little bit more if we were to get over the line. We knew ourselves we had to up it.

Caroline Currid coming in as sports psychologist was a huge help that year as well. People will know even more about her now that she has been so successful with the Limerick hurlers and Munster Rugby, and she was top quality to work with back then as well. She'd come to training sessions and observe. But we rarely had a big meeting with everyone there and Caroline at the top of the room making a PowerPoint presentation. It was more about one-on-ones every couple of weeks; she'd ask how you felt you were going, and after you'd answer she'd give her observations.

Any issues, such as confidence, she'd offer you something, from images of matches in which you'd played well to changing your routine a little, even examples of positive contributions. She'd build a little film of things like that in your head and lift you. That kind of positivity was a huge help. And she could also steer you: 'You know what you have to do' would be one of her directions.

She made a huge contribution when we lost out on our training camp during the National League because of the famous ash cloud in Iceland that year. That was the time of the volcanic eruption which spewed up enough ash to ground flights everywhere, including ours when we were supposed to head for Spain. We were poxed lucky because they got us into Carton House instead, and the weather was nearly better here than in Spain – it was like a foreign training camp anyway. We had an unbelievable week, Sunday to Friday, and halfway through we had a meeting with everyone involved, management and players, that Caroline ran.

She sat us all in a semi-circle and asked us to give our opinions and feelings on losing the All-Ireland final the year before. One by one everyone contributed, and as it went on lads got more and more emotional – they were getting things off their chest about how they felt and how they'd been affected by the experience. It was powerful; you couldn't but be affected by it.

But I had one slight concern while it was going on. I was at the very end of the line, the last person. Fellas, management included, were telling unbelievably powerful stories about meeting their families after the final. Lads were bawling as they recounted them. But I thought, *What am I going to say?* Shane McGrath was two places before me and he spoke very well, but he got upset, obviously, as the memories of the game came back to him. The last before me was Conor O'Mahony, as laid-back a man as you could meet. I was thinking, *He'll be cool here*, but then he broke down listening to Shane, and he stood up and was very honest and open in his contribution. I said my piece – maybe not the most powerful of the meeting – but because we all spoke about it and shared it, the evening had a big effect which lasted all through the season. Classic Caroline Currid.

Funnily enough, Kilkenny didn't come into it as part of

our motivation to do well or to raise standards. Outsiders might have thought that we were saying, or thinking, to ourselves, *We'll get back there and we'll show them*, but I can't remember Kilkenny being mentioned in that context in 2010. The motivation was to achieve for ourselves. They were obviously the standard-bearers at the time, and deep down we probably expected them to get to the All-Ireland final, but we wouldn't have been making those kinds of presumptions with the Munster championship. We wanted to get back to the All-Ireland final and win it, having been so close the year before, and we presumed Kilkenny would be in the final, but those two ideas didn't necessarily connect.

That was the year we found it hard to connect as a team on the field for a while as well. We were down to meet in the first game in the National League, but the snow which fell that day was unbelievable: postponement. (It was the right call. We went up to Dr Morris Park to do a bit of training when the game was called off half an hour before the throw-in and all we could do was some running. You literally couldn't see the sliotar with the snow.) The rearranged fixture was postponed the next day as well, also due to snow and we and Kilkenny moved on to our other league fixtures.

Because we'd played in the All-Ireland final the previous year, there would have been a lot of interest in that rematch in the league and that interest only increased when our opening league game was postponed a couple of times. When the fixture did eventually take place it was a good game. We won 1–14 to 0–13 (Eoin Kelly got the goal that made the difference), which was a boost. The 2009 league final, the 2009 All-Ireland, now this – we were on the way. Getting closer.

What set Kilkenny apart at that stage? The aura they had didn't hurt, being discussed as one of the greatest teams of all time. If they'd put out their second team in that league game and we'd won, we still would have regarded it as significant. Your attitude was different when you played them. Another team might make a couple of changes that would weaken the team, but not Kilkenny. Whatever changes they made, they'd slot a couple of lads in and you knew you still had to be at the top of your game: changes to the team didn't weaken them at all. That was Cody's genius – no matter who the player was, Cody would always get that player's absolute best version of themselves.

The fact that they were regarded as the top dog was something that drove us on at the same time. And we rattled their cage, too – being associated with them in conversations and previews showed that people felt we were closing in on them. And the two counties seemed to be linked in everyone's mind. Around that time it appeared that any time a Kilkenny player was interviewed, then Tipperary were mentioned. We were the closest team to them since Cork had been in All-Ireland finals four or five years earlier.

Mentioning Cork, they were our opponents in the first round of the Munster championship. They had beaten us in the National League, a game played on the Easter bank holiday weekend in Páirc Uí Chaoimh. We stayed on in Clonakilty that evening for a bonding night, as it were.

The day after the bonding most of the lads went home in cars and just a few of us took the team bus, Noel McGrath and John O'Brien included. We were feeling a bit sore in the head, when I got a phone call from a reporter asking if I could answer a few questions. Anything for the distraction, and innocent out, I told him work away, the headache blinding me. After a few queries I noticed there was a lot of laughing at the back of the bus which seemed to be echoing down the phone line. John Devane from Clonoulty Rossmore was the reporter asking the questions but he couldn't keep a straight face to ask the awkward ones he was building up to. Ah, the naivety.

The fact that Cork had beaten us in the league wasn't a cause for alarm in and of itself. It was a close game, we only lost by a point or two, and management wouldn't have been panicking. But having said that, we got a glimpse of something in that league game. Aisake Ó hAilpín, Seán Óg's brother, caused us a bit of bother that day at full-forward but he was switched to the half-forward line. He didn't spend that much time in full-forward but I saw enough of him to recognise he was a handful, and he certainly showed that in the championship game that summer – Cork won 3–15 to 0–14, and Aisake was the trump card, causing problems in and around our square.

He certainly caused me bother. He must be six foot six or seven, and while he was strong, that wouldn't be an issue for me. He'd admit himself his hurling wasn't the sharpest at that stage. But he was very long; long arms, very tall, so rangy that he was difficult to defend against. He was definitely the hardest player I ever had to mark regarding getting to grips with him as he was different, compared to other tall or strong players. Cork didn't have to spray the ball to the left or right when he was full-forward, he was an obvious target for them to hit. If their defenders were under pressure, he was a great out-ball for them. Liam came out and took a lot of the blame on himself, but we just didn't perform. Cork launched balls in on top of Aisake, 'Hoggie' was getting the breaks ... the whole thing got away from us, pure and simple. The Cork crowd were hanging over the wire, or so it seemed. Disaster.

I don't think we were complacent. To give management their due, there would never have been a question of us taking our foot off the pedal – we didn't set the world alight in the league and we were focusing on the championship, which meant the defeat was even harder to take. Don't forget, a lot of us were only in our second full year on the senior team (I was just 21) so it wasn't as if we were in the comfort zone after winning an All-Ireland; that's why I don't think complacency was an issue. I was as up for that game as I ever was, but Cork got goals, they got momentum, and it's very hard to stop that kind of train once it gathers steam. It was a chastening experience but one I relied on later for lessons.

We played on the Sunday and nearly all the players stayed in Cork that night. I have a memory that only a few of us came back home on the bus. That was a particular thing about Cork – if we played in Limerick, everyone would be back to Tipp on the bus, but with Cork, lads liked to stay over. Which meant that when the bus came back it was just myself, Noel McGrath and Brendan Cummins and his wife who got off it. Maybe James Woodlock and 'Hotpoint', the kit man, up the front, and the rest of the 54 seats empty.

The players had a couple of drinks the Sunday night, whether in Thurles or Cork. However the season was organised that year, we had a gap of about six weeks to the qualifiers, so we all met up on the Monday as well for a drink. We knew we weren't training on the Tuesday evening. But of course people started off with the 'How could ye win anything going drinking on a Monday?' talk, which always baffled me. How could a couple of drinks on a Monday affect a game you played 24 hours earlier? As for the 'Sure they were all in this pub or that pub' yarns that would go around – Tipperary is so spread out, from Clonmel to Nenagh to Thurles, it's hard for everyone to get together, which was the case even when the lads came back up from Cork on the Monday.

There was probably a gang of us in Thurles and maybe another gang in Nenagh or somewhere else, but the get-together helped us, enjoying each other's company and getting to know one another's personalities. We might have played in an All-Ireland final together but a lot of us didn't know each other all that well at that stage. Even with the team holiday there are wives, girlfriends, officials, a whole other crowd around. Going out on a Monday like that, it's just the players, lads cutting the back off each other. I'd have heard a lot about Aisake that Monday, for instance – and lads are getting friendlier. By the time training comes around on the Wednesday or Thursday of a week like that, fellas from rival clubs are definitely closer and more willing to back each other up because they know each other better. In the long run it stood to us, definitely.

And management would have known about it too, absolutely. Liam, Eamon and Mick were always well able to gauge the mood in the group and knew when to say, 'Ye worked hard, it didn't go our way today but go on away out, enjoy the night – but don't overdo it, don't draw any trouble and stay together as a group.'

In any event there was a team meeting called for Horse and Jockey that Tuesday evening: management, players, backroom, everyone sitting in a big circle. One senior player stood up and said we shouldn't have gone out the day before, the Monday, that we needed to get back on track. But my impression was that management weren't too bothered about it, that in fact they thought we might have needed a day like that. We'd been building and building and then the thing had collapsed, and blowing off a bit of steam might have relaxed everyone. The meeting ran along lines that would be familiar to lads who've been in team meetings all over Ireland – we could have done this or that better, that some lads weren't quite as fit as they'd been the previous season. The usual.

It wasn't as if Liam and Eamon were giving out or telling us what we had to do. They were more facilitators at that meeting than anything, creating an environment where someone could say to me, 'Pádraic, your standards were far higher last year – are you going to the ball wall as much this year, are you missing the odd gym session?' That keeps people on their toes, but it's not about coming in to the meeting to cut the back off some fella or to call someone names. That's not achieving anything.

In these meetings you should be able to say to another panellist, 'Are you doing everything this year that you did last year?' And a lad might say, 'No, I'm not – my body fat was 12 last year and it's 15 this year,' or 'I've missed a couple of gym sessions.' After a good meeting like that, everyone leaves with the feeling that they've got everything off their chest. At the end, Eoin Kelly stood up and gave a speech that summed the whole thing up, a great speech; he was a senior player and the captain of the team, and he always knew the right note to strike. He'd have the craic as much as anyone but he's one of those lads who can turn it and make things serious – and of course he always backed up what he said by his actions on the field.

There was a lot of honesty in the meeting and we benefited hugely from it. Rather than lads getting hurt by the straight talking, they took inspiration from it, and by the end of it were nearly coming out the door licking their lips and asking when the next training session was planned for. Everyone was lifted, and after that meeting, training really took off.

The criticism was flowing in Tipperary but management were focused on improving the team, not listening to the noise outside. Improvement led to changes. Bonner Maher came onto the team, for instance, and I was shifted out the field from full-back to the half-back line. Gearóid Ryan came in, Mickey Cahill was in the corner.

The qualifier route was all or nothing for us. We played Wexford in the first qualifier and my main memory is of the wrestling match between Declan Fanning and Stephen Banville at the Killinan End. Declan had his helmet torn off his head and when we went in at half-time it wasn't a pretty sight – his ear was hanging off his head and Eamon O'Shea got very emotional about it inside in the dressing room. Declan was a warrior for Tipperary for years, a man I admired as a player and later as a coach, and to see the wound he had, you could nearly fit your fist through it. We wanted to go out and make sure we got through to the next round for his sake as much as anything else.

The changes worked well. We beat Wexford, and the team was becoming more settled. I had been comfortable enough in at full-back but after the Aisake game there was a narrative that I couldn't play there at all, but that was a once-off event, a single game. In any event, I was back out in the half-back line and as happy to be there so long as I was playing. There were other changes visible as well if you looked hard enough. Against Wexford, Bonner went through at one stage – head down, driving hard – and he had Larry and Eoin on either side, a three-on-two. Bonner took on the shot but didn't score, and Larry and Eoin weren't shy afterwards about telling him he should have passed to one or the other. That showed a change in mindset in the group: if there was a better option available, it was all about what was best for the team.

To give Bonner his due, I'd say it was one of the only times in his career he didn't lay the ball off to another player in a better position, but he learned from that experience as well. He was different to Noel, Eoin, Larry, who were all similar enough forwards: great movement, good touch, deadly accurate if they got a yard. And then there was Bonner, smashing into those rucks and coming out with the ball, challenging backs and harassing them when they were trying to come out to clear. He brought a different dynamic to the forward line, winning possession, laying it off, winning frees. If you asked opponents from any county they'd probably say he was one lad they hated marking, but he was a good test for me, I'd been marking those deadly accurate forwards in training with Tipperary and they were one sort of challenge. Bonner came right at you again and again with real physicality, and if you could stand up to that in training, you knew there wasn't a forward any county could throw at you who would be harder to contain. And the Tipp supporters loved him because they saw everything he brought to the team (thankfully he'd tidied the hair up to a certain extent at that stage).

We played Galway in the quarter-final, a day when it could have all come undone. They were very good, but we had that tougher mindset from the meeting in the Jockey and the Cork defeat. Gearóid Ryan had a great day for us against Galway, and from a Thurles perspective the winner was created by the Sarsfields; Pa Bourke came on and set up Larry's winning point. Back in an All-Ireland semi-final.

Larry is a few years older than me, so we wouldn't really have known each other growing up. In 2010 I'd been on the Tipp team two years but I'd also been on the Sarsfields senior team a few years, so we were getting to know each other better, and he was a huge help to me, Pa and Mickey Cahill. The four of us went to training together, to matches together, to the gym together. My home place is out beyond Larry's and Pa is just over the wall, so it was no bother to fall in together. Larry was great to advise us. He'd been there since 2001 so he knew how to direct us – and we were probably good for him and the more experienced lads too, new players bringing in a fresh outlook.

It became a routine for us, particularly if we were playing in Dublin. We'd call to him in the home place in Willowmere Drive and his mother Breda, God rest her, would be having a laugh with us. By the time you'd head out to go to an All-Ireland semi-final or whatever you were laughing and joking away, the mood would be very good. Larry's form was fantastic over those few years – he was in the running for hurler of the year practically every season. (And we helped him along the way. Early on we had a mandatory gym session on Mondays at six up in Tom Kennelly's gym near the Devil's Bit, no excuses. Larry would say, 'Ring me at half five, because if you don't, I won't go – make me go.'

So I'd get onto him every time, because he didn't love the gym. Which he'd tell you himself.)

We had no problem focusing on Waterford in the semi-final, not so much because they were coming in as Munster champions but because they'd turned us over in the 2008 semi-final. We were also on a high after winning the Munster under-21 final the previous year, so there was a bit of a buzz building in the county. We had seven points to spare at the end – Lar chipped in with his usual goal – but the real highlight for me was marking Ken McGrath when he came in at wing-forward, one of his last games for Waterford. Ken was one of my heroes growing up, a fantastic hurler, so I got to say I marked him. He got a point, which initially annoyed me, but then I thought, *That's Ken McGrath I'm marking*. I didn't mind too much.

Making it back to the All-Ireland final was great, obviously, but it was also a help that we'd been there only 12 months beforehand. You know what to expect: not so much the game, but the circus that goes on around it. Getting suits for the All-Ireland final, for instance, is a bit of fun, but it can also be a distraction if it's not handled properly. For us that year it was a tap on the shoulder in training; 'Go on down there to the dressing room', and we got measured, and that was it. Far better than the old way, where you had to go into the shop and stand around and wait and chat. Now it was two minutes of measurements and the next time you thought of the suit was when you picked it up in your hotel room.

The tickets were the same. You'd get a message asking how many tickets you wanted, you were allowed a certain number of complimentary tickets but you could buy more. Reply to the message and then one evening at training Tim Floyd, the secretary, would hand you an envelope. All done.

I never had issues with tickets in that sense. I'd hand my mother the envelope and she'd sort people out. Those might sound like small things, but you'd be surprised how those small things can eat into your preparation if they're not handled properly, how they can distract you.

I had watched the other All-Ireland semi-final, Kilkenny versus Cork, and so I'd seen Henry get injured. Obviously we were trying to get our own house in order and were concentrating on that, but it was impossible to completely shut out the hype. It would have been building anyway with the talk about Kilkenny winning five in a row and so on. Then Henry got injured but he was getting rehab and there was a chance he'd play, and we were hearing about the huge crowds at training in Nowlan Park, and so on.

We were aware of all of that but we were also happy with

our own siege mentality, reaching back to the criticism we'd received after the Cork defeat. Apart from one night, the traditional open evening before an All-Ireland final, we had nobody at training sessions and that suited us fine. A couple of Kilkenny players have said since that the build-up got away from them a little, understandable enough given they were looking at five titles in a row.

We believed we had the beating of them, and going back to the meeting in Carton House, we wanted to remedy the feelings of disappointment after the previous year's All-Ireland final. It wasn't about stopping them winning five in a row. We had our own motivation. That was the feeling in the back of our minds that year – righting our own disappointment by winning the All-Ireland. People say now that you can't bring too much emotion to a big game but I felt we played that one right when it came to the mix of emotion and focus, certainly. 'Ice in the veins' was Eamon O'Shea's saying, and I think we got that balance right in the final that year.

In Croke Park, the experience of the previous year was a help. I felt the roar was louder, if anything, than in 2009 but it didn't come as a shock because I'd been there before. The fact that Henry was playing genuinely didn't become a distraction for us. There was certainly no talk of 'test him out early on' or anything. People forget that John Tennyson was in a similar boat with a cruciate, and the fact that he was named to start as well made us think, *Well, they must be right if they're both on the team*. In fact, I think Liam may have said that week, 'I hope they're all playing so we beat them with the full team rather than giving any excuses.'

A few minutes in I saw Henry pull up, and I could see he was goosed. A couple of the Tipperary players went over to him as he was injured, gave him a tap as he left the field. The Tipp supporters applauded him as he went off, which is something I'll never forget. The rivalry was really warming up at that stage but it was obvious how much respect people had for everything Henry had achieved in the game even then, and he was a legend of the game to me too.

We had our own danger man who was absolutely buzzing that year. Larry was getting goals and floating around doing damage all through that season. He was energised, and an energised Larry Corbett is a dangerous proposition. The first goal he got, out-fielding Noel Hickey and turning and scoring, was significant because I can remember feeling an absolute surge of confidence when he got it. I was thinking, *We're well able for this*. Like every team, we were keen for an early goal, and there it was, working out just as we hoped. The forwards were really showing the benefit of Eamon's coaching by then. That was his third full season with them and they understood what he wanted, they were all on the same wavelength. Their movement also gave us freedom in getting the ball to them, which was a big O'Shea mantra. He'd be in the dressing room saying, 'Just get the ball in, get the ball in.'

And there it was. Shane McGrath turned and got the ball in as he turned, because he knew there'd be someone in there. Lar was on his own at the edge of the square with Noel, and all the other forwards had dragged the Kilkenny backs outfield through their movement. Larry caught the ball, turned and scored a goal.

Kilkenny didn't die. They got back to within a point with Richie Power's goal before half-time, but our confidence was high. In the dressing room someone mentioned the previous year, and it was stressed that that wouldn't happen again and that we'd do whatever it took to win.

In the second half we felt we were on top without dominating on the scoreboard, but the dam-burst was bound to come. You could see the balance of emotion and coolness when Noel McGrath got his goal – he and Eoin were pointing at their heads to keep each other focused.

The real breakthrough was Noel hand-passing to set Larry up for his second goal, and the icing on the cake was to come in the closing stages. Séamus Hennessy came off the bench and got a point, Séamus Callanan came in and had two points almost immediately, Benny Dunne came in to hit a point … It always felt like we'd win, whatever the scoreboard might say. Everything was going our way. David Young came on and hit Eoin Larkin a shoulder, and even though he got a yellow card, that underlined the focus.

The final whistle was everything I imagined it would be. People had been building Kilkenny up, we'd lost the previous year and it had been nearly ten years since Tipperary had won. There's no describing it, and I'll never forget the roar when the game ended. The following year, 2011, I was at the Kerry–Dublin football final with a couple of pals, and there was a huge roar at the final whistle that day too: it felt like the stadium was shaking.

'Bet you've never witnessed anything like this,' I said to the lads with me.

'We did,' they said. 'After last year's final against Kilkenny.'

The following Saturday the week got even better. How? We beat Galway in the All-Ireland Under-21 final, in

Thurles, in front of over 20,000 people, all bouncing with energy from the week just passed. It was party mode in Tipperary that week and the icing on the cake for me was being captain of the under-21 team, which is something I was and am very proud of. You couldn't dream up a better week if you tried.

A shock departure

There was definitely more of spotlight on us in 2011, and you could sense that when playing teams in the league. I won't say we cruised to the Munster final, but there was plenty of confidence in the group.

It was a shock that Liam and the lads went, absolutely. I remember getting the text in October 2010, a few weeks after the All-Ireland – it was Larry who sent me the message:

You're not going to believe what's after happening.

When I saw that I was expecting to hear someone had died, but then he just said it:

Sheedy's gone, the three of them are gone.

It was pure shock. After the 2009 final coming so close, winning in 2010 and winning the under-21 the same year, you thought automatically, *We'll go again next year*. The momentum was building.

Then that text ... everyone on the panel was in shock. It was interesting to get Larry's perspective on the whole thing at that stage, because by then he'd been on the panel for ten years and he'd seen the ups and downs – the unsuccessful years as well as the high points. He'd built a good relationship with Liam and Eamon in particular; they'd got the set-up right, Larry and the older lads had bought into it, there'd been a fresh intake of newer players. For the likes of Larry, it would have been a huge blow.

I was only 21, so while I was stunned, I was still a relative newcomer to the scene. I was concentrating on the following year anyway, on getting back to training and preparing for another season. What people might have missed at the time was the fact that the three of them all left together. In a situation like that, you'll often see one of the management team stays on and offers some continuity. But the three lads had built up such a bond that it was all in or all out – we're a group and we'll stick or twist together.

My own memories of the time were regret that they'd gone because not only were they great people in their own right, they'd organised such a good set-up: everyone was pulling together and the atmosphere was great. I'd go so far as to say that at first I was disgusted. That's feeling selfish as a player and wanting Tipperary to be successful, but of course they have their own lives to lead too. Cian O'Neill, though, stayed on for 2011, which certainly was a help, but you couldn't help but think at the time, *The whole thing is so professional, so well-run, who's going to come in now and lift this to another level again?* And that kind of thinking was probably unfair to Declan Ryan, who replaced Liam. No matter what he and his group did, there was bound to be a sense of hangover, because whatever they brought in, players were going to think, *Well, that's not Sheedy and the lads doing that.*

There was another nagging thought that would hit me, something I still think about now, seeing the likes of John Kiely and how successful he's been with Limerick over a period of five or six years. I go back to 2010 when that thought was: *Are we really on the cusp of something if the management are bailing out when we win an All-Ireland?*

Looking back, you'd have to wonder what might have happened if the lads had stayed in place that time. Would we have won more?

When Declan came in we knew who he was, obviously enough. The first time I can remember him as a player was the 1997 All-Ireland final, Tipp v Clare, and in 2001 he was the senior figure when Tipp won the All-Ireland. I can remember – as a lot of people would in Tipperary – the famous photograph of Declan before the first-round game that year when he was pictured between the two youngsters in the Tipperary forward line, Eoin Kelly and Larry. Declan had his arms around them as a kind of father figure. That was his last year with Tipperary but he was an iconic figure in the county, winning All-Ireland medals in three different decades – 1989, 1991 and 2001 – and we experienced him as a manager with the minors in 2007.

Declan had a presence about him, but he was different to Liam. Declan wasn't constantly in your ear about your performance, whereas Liam would be talking all the time in training to encourage you or to buck you up. Declan didn't show that energy, that's not his personality and I'd say players found that a big change. Liam was always on to you at training, ringing you, one-on-ones, while Declan was more inclined to stand back. Maybe a more old-fashioned approach.

He brought in Tommy Dunne and Michael 'Glossy' Gleeson from the Sarsfields with him. It might have been a little unfair on them because there was such a connection between the team and the previous management, and players were conscious of the difference. In fairness, Tommy did the coaching and he's someone who's always full of energy anyway, very intense. So that was the trade-off between Declan being more reserved than Liam – Tommy was all go, always wanted that bit more from players in training.

Early on, at a team meeting, the new management told us they weren't coming in to make big changes: they said they wanted to continue on with what we were doing. And while we mightn't have been quite as free-flowing, we were still going well in 2011. We won the Munster championship pretty handily on the famous day Larry got 4–4 against Waterford down in Páirc Uí Chaoimh, and then went on to beat Dublin by four or five points in the All-Ireland semi-final. I felt I was at my absolute peak at that time, hurling with freedom.

Afterwards people said they could see the cracks in our win over Dublin, but that didn't take a couple of things into consideration, like the fact that that was a very good Dublin side. They'd won the league that year beating Kilkenny and were there or thereabouts under Anthony Daly; a couple of years later they should have made an All-Ireland final. We mightn't have played that well against them but we were back in the decider.

A few Kilkenny players have said since that they were coming back hard to get us in 2011. That's something we could identify with, obviously enough; we only had to cast our own minds back 12 months and we were in exactly the same situation, just waiting to have a crack off one particular team. In 2010 we'd taken it one game at a time, but that was certainly in the back of our minds: we'll get to see them the final again and have a right go at them. The energy feeds into a siege mentality, and no matter what lads may think – that it might be better to be more open, say – it has to help with the focus.

They showed it too, straight away – they tore into us from the very start that day. On one level that's no great shock, it's an All-Ireland final, after all. But I could tell we didn't have the same energy we'd had in 2010 or 2009, while theirs was different. Can you tell that beforehand, whether the energy isn't at the level required? I can't say I noticed anything in particular that was wrong before the game. Speaking for myself, I thought the build-up was good, even if we hadn't been as fluent in the semi-final as we would have liked. All along we'd have felt things were going well, but if you were to be totally honest, were we flowing as well as we'd been the two previous seasons? Probably not. The obvious question is why not, and if you could answer that … Anyone who's played a team sport knows when it's just right, and when it's just not quite right. If you could nail that difference down in advance, you'd be a millionaire.

Kilkenny's goals were the difference. In the first half Michael Fennelly burst through the middle and got one, just before the break. He was excellent for Kilkenny that year, driving them on from the centre of the field – he bossed us a little bit in that game, he showed that presence. In the second half Eddie Brennan took off on a solo, passed to Richie Hogan, who controlled well, in fairness, before getting their second goal. Pa Bourke pulled one back for us but we never really looked like we were in control of the game, to be honest.

Afterwards I heard plenty of people saying that Eddie Brennan was put on me to move me all over the field and quieten me. Unfortunately for the conspiracy theorists pushing that idea, our own management moved me first, at half-time, to pick up Henry Shefflin because he was causing problems for us. Then again, that's something you just have to listen to. Ever since I finished playing I've heard fellas saying, 'Oh, this player was in big trouble with the lad he was marking,' and sometimes I'm thinking, *What match is this guy watching?* Maybe it's easier if you've just come out of the game to catch those things, but at the time I wouldn't have paid much attention to that kind of talk. Hearing fellas say this player or that player was put on me to run me around …

I can remember Ger Loughnane saying back around 2009 that the Tipperary defence was very slow, that if you turned us we'd be in trouble, which was a narrative I had heard a few times over the years, that if a team got us running back towards our own goal, or ran at us, we were going to struggle. In all honesty I don't think I was burned for pace over the years. I marked some of the fastest lads in the game. Cork ran us around the place a few times, but if the likes of Shane Kingston or Robbie O'Flynn or Eddie Brennan ran at any defender they'd look slow. Then there's the other line, that such-and-such a defender or defence doesn't like forwards running at them. There wasn't a defender that ever liked a forward running at him. Lads like Diarmaid Byrnes and Seán Finn are as good as any, but if Robbie O'Flynn ran at one of them they wouldn't enjoy it. No back would.

It was a lazy narrative to throw that at the Tipperary defence. The Kilkenny defence had a hard day at the office with our forwards but that accusation wasn't thrown at them, and that's understandable when you win games, because the win excuses everything. Even though the winning backs don't like being run at any more than the losing backs!

There were subtle differences between 2009 and 2011, even though the end result was the same. In 2009 we were heartbroken, but there was the comfort once the dust settled of knowing that we'd emptied ourselves, that we'd given a fair account of ourselves collectively. In 2011 we knew we hadn't performed as well as a team, and that solace we'd had in 2009 wasn't there. Looking at the Kilkenny lads celebrating afterwards out on the field, we had regrets certainly, and the fact that we hadn't given a good account of ourselves was a big part of those regrets.

A couple of years afterwards Tommy Walsh said in an interview that he felt we'd over-celebrated the 2010 All-Ireland win out on the field at the final whistle, and I thought, *Hang on a second, that was our first All-Ireland as a team after beating one of the best teams of all time.*

I didn't have any bone to pick with them celebrating in 2011, though. I could see what it meant to them. They wanted to get back to the final and have a go off us, they did that and they were good enough to win. Fair play to them, they were entitled to celebrate.

I could see what Tommy meant, and how you could use that as fuel, but quite apart from Kilkenny, my feeling that time was disappointment that we hadn't played up to our potential and given a good account of ourselves. The 'over-celebrating' narrative – that that was the reason we didn't put All-Irelands back to back – didn't stand up to examination. How could a team that overdid its celebrations come back and win the Munster final by a cricket score and reach the All-Ireland final?

It was annoying, because we were disappointed that we hadn't realised our potential, not that we hadn't won two All-Irelands in a row. Honestly, that was something that didn't come up in discussions within the group. I met Ger Loughnane at the *Irish Daily Star* awards a few years later, after 2016. We got on well, there were no problems, but he felt he had to tell me that we'd have to win All-Irelands back to back to be considered a great team. But that never became a focal point. (Ger's Clare side of the 1990s didn't win All-Irelands back to back and they're certainly considered a great team.) I have a vague memory of Eamon O'Shea mentioning it in passing in 2019 but it was never a big deal for us as a group, certainly not as big a deal as it was outside the group. I never went back in January thinking, *This year we have to do it for the two in a row*; I went back every year thinking we have to do it because it's a new year, and that's what we expect of ourselves. Our standards meant that we believed we'd go close to an All-Ireland every year. Regardless of the results the previous season.

Looking back at 2011, I can recall the 'I saw it coming' talk after the final – people saying they weren't surprised we lost because of the way things had been going all year. (Though funnily enough, few of them were talking like that after the Munster final.) That was irritating, but to be fair there wasn't much negativity. Disappointment, yes, but getting so close to another All-Ireland kept a lot of criticism at bay. It was the following year when it became really negative.

Treading water, making enemies

Cian O'Neill was gone after 2011, which was a difference straightaway. The strength and conditioning coach is probably the member of the backroom team in any county side that the players deal with most, so it's a vital appointment. At the time Cian was at the absolute top of his game, a demanding coach, always looking for more from you, who was so good that you went along with everything he wanted because you knew you'd get the benefits from that work.

But again, like the management itself, when he left, players started thinking about what he did and started comparing the new man's approach to his. Ross Dunphy was the man Declan brought in, an army man, and he was good. The effort was certainly there from all concerned, but we were still making that comparison, unfair though it was.

We were still winning. We got through Munster well and won the Munster final by seven points. On the surface it was business as usual. Two Munster titles in a row isn't something to sniff at, and Tipperary would welcome that kind of record now. But beneath the surface it was different. Standards slipped a little. Fellas weren't doing everything they could do, taking a couple of shortcuts. That can happen, particularly if players don't feel that they're being pursued the whole time to do the right thing. And this year the cracks became visible. We beat Limerick in Semple Stadium but it was a struggle; we beat Cork narrowly; we beat Waterford in that Munster final but despite what the scoreboard would suggest – 2–17 to 0–16 – it was of a piece with the championship as a whole. We were doing enough to get over the line, and that was about it. But it was still enough to get us into an All-Ireland semi-final. Against Kilkenny.

Games were fixed in the county championship in

Tipperary for a couple of weeks before that All-Ireland semi-final. Those games were important for the club championship – we had to win against Loughmore to progress, for instance. But on the Thursday or Friday before those games were played, Tipperary brought us down to Bere Island in west Cork for training, and they didn't spare us. Those training trips are always a chance for the management to get a lot of work done with the panel in a short amount of time, and they certainly took that chance. Army-style training, getting woken up in the middle of the night, running up mountains – the whole thing.

Lads were broken up by the time we got back home to Tipperary for the weekend – and then we had to go out and play competitive games in the club championship that Sunday. I booked in with Mick Clohessy, our physio and masseur, to try and get the legs back the night before our game against Loughmore, and there were lads who had bigger problems to deal with: Eoin Kelly got badly injured in the South final afterwards and another few lads picked up knocks. Not ideal in the run-up to playing Kilkenny for a place in the All-Ireland final, and again, you couldn't help thinking that it wouldn't have happened in previous years.

I wasn't sure what the management thought process was in 2012. Was it to knock some softness out of the team?

It didn't help. Eoin's injury meant he didn't train fully or properly, in the lead up to the semi-final, and other players were carrying knocks as well. That all showed in the game when it came – as had happened all year, we did enough in the first half and actually led at the break, but we weren't flowing.

We led 1–10 to 1–9 but Brendan Cummins had to make a couple of good saves in the first half to keep us in it. And our goal came when Larry challenged David Herity for the ball and it broke for Pa Bourke rather than being created by us moving the ball around ourselves, the way Kilkenny did when they got their goal through Richie Power. At half-time we weren't saying, 'We've a right chance here,' but at the same time we were winning the game. It wouldn't be unheard of for a team to improve in the second half, obviously, and take over. But then …

Everyone can probably remember what happened in the second half, or certain parts of it with Jackie Tyrrell waiting for Larry by the tunnel, and the two of them – and Pa Bourke and Tommy Walsh – running around Croke Park, not even paying attention to the match but trying to switch markers.

Understandably enough, that became a lot of people's focus after the game, which was no surprise given that it was a lot of people's focus during the game itself. I didn't really notice it was going on. I was concentrating on my own job, and the side-show was taking place in the far corner of the field. The odd roar from the crowd could be heard which bore no relation to what was happening in the game itself, but in that second half we had plenty to focus on ourselves at the back, because the whole year came to a head, really, in that last 35 minutes.

Whatever unhappiness was in the team with the club games, the injuries, and then the circus with the lads running around, Kilkenny hit us for 3–15. It was a surreal experience, because we'd won and lost close games against Kilkenny for the previous couple of years, and to be beaten like that was bizarre. There was no great post-mortem in our dressing room afterwards. We wanted to clear out and get home.

That was also the game in which I clashed with Michael Rice on the sideline under the Hogan Stand. I didn't take any notice of it during the game – he was gone off the field within a few seconds, while I was jogging back into position. It was only a few days later that I realised there was so much talk about it. I watched it back because it had happened so fast in the game that I'd barely noticed it. And looking at it, I thought I went in hard but not dirty. I was open enough going into the challenge, using one hand, but if I'd had the two hands on the hurley I wouldn't have made it to the ball at all. The hurleys clashed and mine slid up his stick and hit his fingers, but I didn't deliberately go for his hand. In that situation you have a split-second decision to make and I went hard for the ball because if I didn't, I'd have been in bother myself.

I appreciate that going in one-handed like that, you're leaving yourself open to doing some damage, but I think anyone watching would say that I didn't go in to 'do' him. He didn't hit the ground, he just walked off, which I hadn't really noticed during the game itself. But later a couple of people said I was getting stick about it, and then there was a bit of a rigmarole about me not contacting him to see how he was. I texted him saying 'Jesus I didn't realise it was that serious' and in fairness he texted me back, but it stayed in people's heads.

I'd have heard since that some Kilkenny players supposedly lost respect for me after this incident. That's fine, that's up to them, but I can truthfully say without hesitation that I didn't go out to hurt Michael in that instance, despite what those few might think. I have tremendous respect for Kilkenny and their former manager, as readers can see from this book.

Later in that game I swung back loosely on T.J. Reid when we were being destroyed and I was absolutely frustrated. I was coming out with the ball and felt he was hanging on to me, so I drew back and swung out in frustration. I wasn't sent off – I didn't really connect with him – but with that one I'd hold my hands up. I shouldn't have done it and wouldn't have had any complaints if I'd been given red. But with Michael Rice I couldn't understand it – I'd genuinely gone for the ball and hurt him accidentally. If you went through the film of those games you'd see plenty of hits and belts given out on both sides, but there seemed to be an awful lot of attention paid to that one incident.

We went right into the club campaign afterwards. We had a good run, winning the Munster club championship, and I was captain, so I'd parked Tipperary once we hit the autumn. Then I got a text again, not too long after the semi-final: Declan and the lads had met the county board and had decided to step away. There were no players' meetings to discuss the management situation – or if there were, I wasn't invited to them – and I didn't go to meet Tim Floyd, the county board secretary, to give him my views on the situation. I was vice-captain that year but I was still young enough.

I would say that Declan and the lads felt the thing was getting away from them and decided to go, but of course that meant there was a vacancy. And the worries began all over again.

Who were they going to bring in as manager? One of the other players texted me soon after.

I'm hearing Eamon O'Shea could be interested in coming back as manager.

Really? But then there was no word at all for a week or two, and you ended up thinking it was just another rumour. All of a shot, though, it was happening. I bumped into a county-board official, who said it was true that Eamon was coming back once he ironed out one or two small details.

And immediately we thought, *Great*. We were rattling along well with the club knowing that when that finished up we were going back in with O'Shea. Mick Ryan would be back with him, and Paudie O'Neill was coming in once it was confirmed. We were delighted. As a manager he was still also the coach, more or less. Looking back now, was that too much for one man to take on, did it put too much pressure on him? Maybe, but he was back and he brought that energy back with him.

And the players responded. Eamon is a shrewd operator. He might be based in Galway but he'd have had plenty of eyes and ears around Tipperary keeping tabs on what lads were up to. Mick Ryan lived locally, so he'd drop in on gym sessions to see if the players were on track. And they were. The players were definitely energised by the new management … and the new strength and conditioning coach.

Lukasz Kirszenstein had been involved as an assistant in previous years, putting the programme into operation. That meant he was the man in the gym with us most nights. When he became the chief strength and conditioning coach, with full control, he had a huge influence on us. He changed my thinking about S&C and my body certainly changed from working with him, something quite a few other players would probably say as well. I still can't understand how Tipperary let him get away to Galway at the end of 2016 – that was a huge mistake. He was great to work with, always available to give you some advice or to tweak your programme, and he always hit the right note. You could have a bit of craic with him, great company, but he never had a problem telling fellas to put in a bigger effort. He'd say to me straight out, 'That's good, Paudie, but you should be lifting more than that, or lifting heavier. You're talking too much instead of lifting and doing your work, come on.'

Out of respect for him, for his ideas and his own work

rate, you'd do that work no problem. Taking my lead from him, while I'd always taken my training very seriously, I went up another level. Away from the group training sessions I'd go for a run or do another session in the gym. And I went crazy with my nutrition. My body fat dropped to 7–8 per cent, and I saw the negative effect: I started getting tired very easily and my energy levels weren't near what they should have been. When Lukasz saw our scan results he was straight over to me in the gym: 'Paudie, you're not a boxer, you're a hurler, bring that body fat percentage up a bit.' I thought the lower my body fat was, the better, but that wasn't the case and eventually I found a happy medium. He brought my game to another level when it came to physical preparation.

This was the year I also made the hut behind Mick Clohessy's house my second home. Mick was our masseur with both Tipp and Sars for all my career, and I'd have ventured out the week of every game to get a once-over from Mick to make sure all was up to scratch. As the years went on this increased to twice a week. Mick is a great friend to this day and had a major part in ensuring I played most of my career without injury.

For all that, we never really got going in 2013. We lost the league final to Kilkenny in Nowlan Park – a bad omen, as it turned out – with Michael Fennelly getting a couple of goals. We weren't much better in the championship: Limerick beat us in the Gaelic Grounds and we were in the qualifiers. Kilkenny in Nowlan Park. That was different for a number of reasons. Kilkenny had gone out against Dublin in the semi-final of the Leinster championship, so they were on a mission to get back on track, and I'm sure when they saw the draw they smelled blood, that there was a sense of 'Whatever happens, this crowd aren't going to beat us.' Then you had the fact that the game was on in Nowlan Park. Kilkenny don't play a lot of big championship games there, so there was a novelty factor, and it was against their main rivals of the previous few years. The crowd was there for hours before the throw-in, and there ended up being over 22,000 in the ground. If you've been in Nowlan Park you'll know that there's not much room if that many are squeezed in there.

And in fairness, they played that atmosphere really well. Before the game there were a few lads named on the team that hadn't been on the team announced earlier in the week – the likes of Paul Murphy and T.J. Reid came in – and then Henry Shefflin, who was coming back from surgery, was listed among the subs, and the roar when his name was called out over the PA ... they were baying for blood at that stage. It wouldn't have bothered us, but you couldn't help but be aware of the reaction of the crowd, the way they were being stoked up even more. And because of the noise from the supporters the Kilkenny players were probably getting energised as well, even though it wasn't a great season for them overall.

We did well, however. Larry was absolutely going to town on their defence early on, he was terrific. If he had stayed on the field we'd have beaten them, I think, and you could tell that he worried their backs; he always asked a different question of their defence. After 20 minutes I was thinking, *Larry is on fire, we're going to win well here*. He had a goal and his confidence was flying as a result. And then, disaster: he pulled the hamstring and had to come off. What always stays with me from that game, though, is the contrast between the treatment he got going off the field that day and the reaction of the Tipperary supporters in 2010 when Henry's cruciate went again in the All-Ireland final. That day Tipp lads showed great sportsmanship in clapping Henry off the field, but I'll never forget the jeers Larry got going around the outside of the pitch in Nowlan Park in 2013. I wasn't too impressed with that.

The game came down to a chance Eoin Kelly got late on, but J.J. Delaney came jumping across and made himself big, and the ball came off his elbow. When something like that happens you definitely get the idea that it isn't going to be your day, and sure enough Kilkenny pulled away.

It was an opportunity lost. The next day out, Kilkenny lost to Cork in Thurles, so they weren't flying it themselves. It was a disappointing year because everything had been building well, we'd made it to the league final and yet here we were, barely into July, and gone. The club lost early in the championship as well; we'd made it to the All-Ireland club semi-final earlier in the year but we were unable to keep that going.

There was one silver lining, however. After the loss to Kilkenny on the Saturday afternoon, the following Thursday morning myself, Brian 'Buggy' O'Meara and Brendan Maher were on a flight to New York to play hurling for the rest of the summer.

New York: blisters in the sun

It was an unusual summer for me because from the age of 17 I'd been hurling through to September every year, more or less, either with Tipperary or the Sarsfields. I hadn't been settled with work that time either. I went to the University of Limerick to do a fitness course in 2012, but Eamon O'Shea, to give him his due, had lined up some work for me with KN, who were contractors for Irish Water, in 2013. It was a handy job for hurling, and

I was grateful to Eamon for arranging it, but it was a stopgap.

On the Monday after we lost to Kilkenny I got a phone call asking me to come out to play for Tipperary (New York), and I wasn't going to turn it down. I could recognise the opportunity for what it was and told the lads in KN I was off and they were grand about it, wished me luck.

We stayed in McLean Avenue in Yonkers, a place familiar to generations of Irish people visiting or living in New York, and we had a great time. That Tipperary crew have looked after me ever since and are some of the biggest supporters of the blue and gold I've met. I've been back a few times since and always enjoyed it, but that was my first time, really, being away from home and I had a lot to learn. For the first week they left us off to our own devices, so we did a bit of exploring of Manhattan – and a bit of partying – but by the second week we were ready to work. I fell in with a furniture manufacturing company – high-end work, mostly for millionaires – so I was fetching and carrying around the workshop for the lads who were doing the actual work. (God love them, a few struggled with my Tipperary accent.)

Outside work we didn't stray too far from the native soil. Brendan Maher from Roscrea has a pub on McLean

Avenue, McKeon's, but McLean Avenue is as Irish as anywhere in Ireland. The people there were terrific to us – they couldn't do enough for you – and when the matches kicked in it was even better. We were full-time transfers, the likes of myself, Brian O'Meara, Donagh Maher, Shane Bourke, John Sheedy, so we had to get 90-day transfers from our clubs back home, while Brendan Maher came out to play at weekends. The only issue was you never knew who you'd be playing against at the weekend. The locals would say, 'We'll beat this crowd handy,' and then before the game you'd find out that there were three or four county players after landing into JFK that morning. The assignment got a bit tougher.

It's funny how fast you get into the routine, though. Work away all week, take it easy on Saturday, then a game on Sunday. But before the game we'd call over to Brendan Maher's house – the man who owned McKeon's – for breakfast, and to watch the games being broadcast from Ireland with the time difference. If there wasn't a game to play, the day could end up going in a different direction altogether. One weekend a few of the Tipp lads in Boston said they'd come down to us, the likes of my cousin Denis, so we paid our ten dollars cover charge and went to the pub to see the games. The downside is you're in the pub at nine in the morning, which makes for a long day. We came out for fresh air after a couple of games and it was melting hot, but yours truly was cute enough to stay under the canopy outside the pub. Unfortunately I wasn't cute enough to keep my legs under the canopy. I was sitting for an hour with the legs dangling in the sun, so when I wanted to get up to go to the toilet I couldn't move. Blisters from hip to ankle. Agony.

We had some right matches over that summer. Galway (New York) were the team to beat but we got to the final and were confident enough. I can remember running out in Gaelic Park and glancing over to see who they had. The first lads I saw were Mick Fennelly and Eoin Larkin. I was thinking, *Am I ever going to get away from these lads, even 3,000 miles from Ireland?* I ended up marking Eoin and had to be tuned in – the last thing you'd want is to get cleaned out in a game like that because that's a story that wouldn't be long getting back to Ireland with plenty of legs on it. We won the game, though. At least we had that.

In fairness, we would have met up with the Kilkenny lads afterwards for a drink, no bother. Paul Murphy, who played for Kilkenny, was over and back that time as well with Long Island and we met him a couple of times after games. But there were plenty of differences. It was so hot, you wouldn't bother having a shower for a good hour after the final whistle. No point. You'd need a shower immediately after the shower, from the sweat. After the game, Therese Crowe, who's from Thurles originally and was helping out with the team, gave us wet towels instead and we put those around our necks, and then a box of beers was wheeled in while we cooled down.

It was an enjoyable summer and a great change of scenery. The crowd I was with were terrific company, and we had some outstanding days and nights, but it was hard to watch the games from so far away. Having been to the final a few times you couldn't help looking at an All-Ireland semi-final and thinking, *If we were there we'd be doing this next week and that the week after.*

I came home the week of the All-Ireland final because I was down to play in the Kilmacud Sevens with Sarsfields the day before the final. When we were out in Yonkers there was never a return date given – 'Lads, ye'll have to go home out of it on this Friday' – and I could see how lads would end up staying there for years after going out for one summer. I'd be a home bird anyway, but once it got to All-Ireland semi-final stage my mind was made up. It was a great way to live for a few months but I was as happy to be heading home. It wasn't real life to me. It was living in a bubble, which was very enjoyable, but not for me long term. I got chatting to a few of the lads out there and more often than not, when I asked how they'd ended up in the States, the answer was the same: 'Like yourself, I came out playing hurling and I just never went back.' I was happy to experience it, and when Ronan, my brother, got a similar opportunity a few years later I encouraged him to take it, because it was a chance that mightn't come around for him again. For myself, I wanted to be back and going to Dr Morris Park two or three times a week for training. I enjoyed New York but I knew what suited me, what I wanted.

I came back without a bob in my pocket – though the blisters had cleared up, thankfully – but I had a fresh appetite for the games. Ready to go again. To that end, I had been on to Lukasz for programmes because I wanted to train hard while I was in the States. He had sent them on to me so I kept ticking over that summer and was ready for training when we resumed with Tipperary.

We were back at the start of November that year – Eamon brought us back that bit earlier – and you could sense there was something new in the group. Gary Ryan, the renowned runner, was in doing the strength and conditioning along with Lukasz and we got gym programmes for November and December – two or three sessions a week – as well as two running sessions a week. We would meet as a group every Saturday for a hurling session. One particular Saturday in the run-up to Christmas we finished our hurling session and had a 1K time trial as a fitness test. I was in good shape and felt I could knock out a good time, which I did, three minutes four seconds. I was happy out until I saw a new lad, Colin O'Riordan, fly it in under three minutes. He's now a professional Australian football player with Sydney Swans, unsurprisingly.

That was a fair amount to take on at that time of the year, but we had been knocked out so early we were keen to get back. We trained fair hard that winter and we got more of a benefit again because lads really looked after themselves in terms of nutrition and rest, all the little things that add up to the big things. Usually November and December are the only months of the year you'd get a chance to go out with your friends whenever you want and wherever you want – presuming your club isn't in the Munster club championship – but that year was different. We were training that November and December instead, and training hard. Some of those Saturday-morning sessions in Dr Morris Park were testing enough, but I felt that block of training really stood to me, and maybe others, for a year or two afterwards.

We were given the Christmas off, but early in the new year we were back. Full speed ahead for 2014.

Watching Bubbles' free: 2014

Everyone bought into it. Everyone. Now, in one sense there was no choice, because it was clear from Eamon and the management that they weren't going to let what happened in 2013 happen again. But we took encouragement from 2013 as well. Clare and Cork were in the All-Ireland final and they'd beaten Limerick and Dublin to get there. We felt that if we got ourselves right we were as good as those teams. We had to up our standards but based on the volume of work we did, even in the winter of 2013, we were confident we'd done that.

First, though, I had to deal with concussion. We were training up in Dr Morris Park one Saturday morning and I went up for a high ball and whatever way I got knocked in mid-air, I fell down and hit my head off the ground. When I got home I started getting sick, and the team doctor, Kevin Delargy, stood me down. I was going to see him every week to pass the concussion test so I could get back, and every week I was thinking to myself, *I'm flying this here*, and every week he was saying to me, 'No, not yet.'

So I didn't play a game for three or four weeks. I felt I was ready but there was no negotiating. He'd say, 'The slightest bump could be serious,' and he wouldn't let me play. There was an advantage to it in that even though I couldn't play, I was able to do another few weeks of hard physical training while I recovered. I'd rather have played the games but my fitness levels were improving at the same time.

I was doing the water bottles for the team in a couple of the league games I missed, and we beat Cork in Thurles in a tight game to reach the semi-final. I got back for that game, against Clare, and we won. In the final it was our old pals Kilkenny. Even enough into extra time, T.J. worked a short sideline to Richie Hogan, Richie back to T.J. for the winning point. Another cracking game. Another narrow defeat.

That was disappointing, but we felt we were going well until we played Limerick in Thurles in the Munster championship. That was the day that ended with Shane Dowling getting a late, late goal to win the game. That was a setback, because we felt we were improving, that our fitness was there, that we had maybe done enough – and then there's a sucker punch right at the very end.

What happened, though, was that the team became more united because of the reaction within the county to the defeat. There was a gap of four or five weeks to the next game because we'd lost so early in the championship, so we went out together that night for a drink, and we went out the following day as well – again, all together as a team. Then the word started to get around that the Tipp team was out having a drink together, and the media got hold of it later that week.

This led to people giving out because supposedly we weren't doing things right and we weren't preparing properly. Yet there was no word about our preparation in the run-up to the game – a game we could have won but for a late goal. The logic of that argument I could never understand: how could whatever we did 48 hours after a game affect what happened in that game? It was brought up in the camp because people were complaining about us going out on the Monday when I presume they wanted us to be getting ready for a game four or five weeks later. I think it was the Wednesday when we met with Eamon and the management, and in fairness to them, they never made a big issue out of it. Their attitude was very much 'Let them say what they want, we'll concentrate on our own job, they can come with us if they want and if they don't want to that's fine too – the loyal ones will stay with us.'

Management pointed out that we had burst ourselves with work since the previous November, we'd been unlucky in the league final, we'd been caught at the death against Limerick ... they said we'd turn it around. And when we got drawn against Galway in the qualifiers, that was our chance to show we could do just that.

People talk about our rivalry with Galway at the All-Ireland semi-final stages, but this was a pretty significant game in itself. (It was a pretty significant game in the Maher household anyway, because it was Ronan's championship debut. It didn't go that well for him in that he was subbed off at half-time, but there were better days ahead for him, thankfully.) I was full-back on Johnny Glynn, and he got

ALL ON THE LINE

two goals the same day – he caught two balls and hit two goals, but I felt I was playing pretty well on him apart from that. James Barry was moved from centre-back to full-back and I went to centre-back. James quietened Glynn and I was able to get on more ball at centre-back, so the moves helped us.

With 20 minutes to go we were six points down, but compared to the previous games we were moving well, and the months of hard training began to come to the fore: we hit 2–10 in the final quarter and pulled away to win by nine points. That was the shot in the arm we needed, and you could tell by the lads coming into the dressing room afterwards that the energy was well and truly back in the team. Eamon was living in Galway so we knew it meant a lot personally, and we were delighted to get the result for him. It was also a game that settled the team. We held that shape for the rest of the year, or almost the rest of the year. The next qualifier was against Offaly and I was named at full-back again. I had thought I'd be playing out the field, but after we won that game to get through to play Dublin in the quarter-final, Eamon moved me back to the half-back line. We beat Dublin to set up a semi-final against Cork. There was a lot of talk about them because they'd been in the All-Ireland final the year before and they'd won

140

the Munster championship by beating Limerick in the last game played in Páirc Uí Chaoimh.

It was ideal for us. The focus was on them, they had momentum behind them, but traditionally we'd have no fear of Cork, and we had some pretty good momentum behind us as well. We won by ten points and Séamus Callanan was excellent that day. He'd been terrific against Galway in the qualifiers and his eye was really in. He got an early goal against Cork to settle us and his second goal finished the game, really. Under Eamon O'Shea, he really kicked on. Up to that year he was on and off the team: nobody doubted his talent, but from that year on he was a real leader.

And the team was beginning to change too. Eoin wasn't a starter any more. John 'Bubbles' O'Dwyer had come in and added another weapon up front. Cathal Barrett was really impressing at the back: he'd done well on Henry Shefflin in the league final so we knew he was at that level, and in the All-Ireland semi-final Patrick Horgan was going through at one stage but Barrett got back to dispossess him and come away with the ball. It was the kind of defending we'd come to appreciate from Cathal in the following years.

It was all coming together, and just at the right time. The final against Kilkenny, the drawn All-Ireland, had everything because both teams were playing with freedom. It'd be almost impossible to go back and list out everything that happened, there were so many incidents. It had the physicality of the previous games but it also had some of the openness we'd seen the year before between Cork and Clare.

To me that drawn game is the greatest All-Ireland final ever played, and we didn't even win it. I always felt we were there with a chance. Kilkenny had a slight advantage, maybe, but we were level a dozen times during the game, so they never got too far ahead of us. T.J.'s goal was a big score for them, but at that stage our experience was a factor as well. We'd been in All-Ireland finals before and knew you never had it all your own way, so when the opposition got the boost of a goal you could keep your concentration.

And our confidence was high after the way the season had turned out. Beating Galway and Cork, for instance, would always boost your confidence, and knowing we were capable of a performance like the one against Cork in the semi-final meant we'd be there or thereabouts. It was a fourth final for most of us, all of them against Kilkenny, so we weren't going to collapse if they got ahead of us. Barrett in particular was a big addition to the defence and 'Bubbles' ability to clip a few points when needed gave us huge confidence; the contrast between that experience and 2012, when the whole thing had fallen down around our ears, was huge. We believed what we were doing and knew our jobs. When people ask about confidence that's what helps – everyone knows what they have to do, and what everyone else has to do. The fitness we worked on so hard in November and December also strengthened our self-belief. We finished very strongly against Galway and against Cork, so we always knew if we were there or thereabouts in the closing stages of the final, we had a chance.

People will remember those closing stages, but we had other chances that day. We left two penalties after us. We were six points up in the first half when we got the first, but Eoin Murphy saved it. The second penalty came with ten minutes to go and scoring that would have been a huge boost to our momentum. Obviously if we'd scored one of those it wouldn't have come down to the last few seconds, when Brian Hogan came upfield with the ball for Kilkenny. I saw him coming into our half, right towards me, and thought to myself, *I'm not moving*. He came at me and I stood my ground; he crashed into me, and the referee gave a free against him.

I was shocked that I'd got a free for barging, and I lost the head a small bit with a few fist-pumps, but it sank in almost immediately. We had a chance to win the game, all of a sudden: *If we put the ball over the bar we could win this game in a minute*, was the way I was thinking, and the way 'Bubbles' was striking the ball in the game and all year, I had no doubt he'd do it, even if it was 100 metres out. I stood behind him as he hit it. Praying.

He struck it sweetly and I followed it all the way, and it looked so good for so long, then … Shit! I couldn't see if it was over or not from where I was standing, and I was out on the field directly in line with the shot, so I don't know if anyone could really tell with the naked eye. We were all waiting around for the screen to flash the message, and I was thinking, *If this says 'Tá' we're All-Ireland champions.*

'Níl'. Then the final whistle went. What can you say?

It was a performance that validated a lot of the work we'd done all year – hard, hard work, that nobody saw. We'd lost the league final by a point after extra time and gone out because of a last-minute goal against Limerick, so the wheels had never come off. If anything, it showed we were very close. People had become negative about the team but the confidence was there among the lads, and that confidence comes from having that hard work done. It's a comfort: you know you've got that in the tank and no matter what happens, you'll be able to go to the end.

And that showed in the final, the way we went so close with that surge in the last ten minutes. We kept driving forward and very nearly snatched it. Not bad for a team that wasn't doing the right things, supposedly, a few weeks beforehand.

The replay got away from us. We led at half-time but never took control of the game, and the two Powers did a lot of damage for Kilkenny, John in particular. He hadn't been playing with Kilkenny long but he was a good introduction by Brian Cody. He's done that a few times over the years, launched a new player into an All-Ireland final or another big game and got a good return from it. He certainly did that day. Pádraig Walsh played instead of his brother Tommy, which was another move that worked out for them. We got a goal late on from Séamus Callanan to cut their lead to two points, so there was hope, but they were on top for most of the game.

My own experience was a mirror of the team's. In the drawn game I was centre-back, picking up Richie Hogan, and I felt I had a good game. I got on a lot of ball and sat back a bit, trying to mind the house and protect the full-back line. Further out, Richie got four or five points from play, though. I thought I'd done fine – I was doing the job I was given – but for the replay there was a small change.

Eamon said to me, 'We'll play you at six but maybe keep more of an eye on Richie.' So I did, and he only got a couple of points – he didn't have nearly the same influence on the game as he had the first day. But the other side of that was I was disappointed in my own performance. I was too focused on nullifying him rather than making more of a contribution to my own team. Fair enough, he didn't do as much damage, but I felt I should have done more.

That's the balance you have to strike at six – sit back and protect your full-back line but let your man clip a couple of points, or track him and blot him out but maybe don't get as involved in the game as much yourself. I remember Donal Óg Cusack did a piece on *The Sunday Game* the day of the drawn game, showing Richie drifting off out into pockets of space to pick off points, while I was sitting back, away from him. That was fine: I had a job to do for the team in that game as well, but it probably played on my mind a bit too much ahead of the replay.

That was disappointing. And no trip to New York after, either! There'd been three weeks between the matches, which was a very long stretch. The day after the drawn match we went to Carton House for recovery, and there was a good buzz around the camp because we'd done so well to almost nick the game, but you couldn't help thinking: *Three more weeks of this, waiting and killing time and mulling the draw over in your mind?* (I wasn't alone, either. At the final whistle the first day I can remember shaking hands with J.J. Delaney, and while we were all up in a heap with the draw, he seemed to be particularly pissed off. I only realised after the replay, when he announced his retirement that he had obviously planned to hang it up after the final but the draw meant he had another couple of weeks of training. I remember thinking after the draw, *That man is absolutely disgusted.* No wonder.)

Preparing for an All-Ireland replay like that is tough on management, because three weeks is a funny enough break between matches. One week is fine, because you don't do anything physical, just recovery, but three weeks – management are probably wondering if they should do some physical work the first week, week and a half, to keep the players ticking over. Everything is built around getting every player at an absolute all-time physical peak the day of the All-Ireland final, and then you have to get them all up to the same level three weeks later. Mentally it's tough too, because you have the attitude that everything will end at half five that first Sunday and you're expecting all that tension to be released. But it doesn't release, and you have to get yourself tuned in all over again.

Kieran McGeeney came in with us as a performance coach in 2014. Eamon invited him in and I found him very good to work with. A great help. One of the best, if not the best, performance coach I've come across in my time. I drove up to Dublin to meet him several times away from the group, and if I told people, they often asked if I was mad, but I got a huge amount out of those meetings — they were well worth the effort. He'd test you straightaway when you'd sit down in the coffee shop.

'What did you do this week? Why did you do that? Why didn't you do this? What have you done to help and improve your team-mates?'

And once I thought about it I realised he was right. That there was more I could be doing. He'd pick up on recovery, nutrition. If we'd played a match the weekend before, he'd ask if I'd watched it back yet, for instance.

'No, not yet.'

'So you haven't taken notes on what you need to take out of it?'

And once I thought about it, I realised he was right. That there was more I could be doing.

It wasn't all confrontation. Kieran can be encouraging — 'Yeah, I see it in you alright' — but he'd always be testing and looking for that bit more from you. He'd pick up on something and say, 'You need to work on that, so do it, and drop me a text tomorrow when you get it done.' I found his approach very good. It wasn't all about kicking you up the backside, it was positive but kept you on your toes, which can be a difficult balance to strike. And I felt I'd been going well, so trying to get up a level or two was a good challenge for me also. Heading to Dublin every two weeks or so to chat to him was a huge benefit to my game that year.

He came to Tipperary to do some team sessions as well, or he'd come to training and keep an eye on what was happening. Sometimes he'd fall in with us for a gym session, and he'd test us there as well. At that stage we would have felt we were going well and were experienced in the gym, but McGeeney would come over, and when you'd see what he'd do you'd end up thinking, *Now that's training hard*. He has huge strength, and he showed us that there was always more. We might be doing chin-ups, and our programme would be to do six. McGeeney would do ten with a chain hanging off him. Or he'd chat about training.

'How do you think your gym work is going, Paudie?'

'Good, yeah. Good.'

'I was in with the UFC lads there last week ...' or 'I was in the SBG Gym a few days ago' – which is owned by John

Kavanagh, the MMA coach – and he'd mention what they were doing, and then you'd end up thinking, *Wait, I can go harder. We're not training at all.*

By sharing that experience he was driving us on. Showing us, not telling us, that you can always do more.

And it was a good contrast with Eamon, who wouldn't be giving out to players. He might say, 'I need you to do a bit more,' but he'd be very much an arm-around-the-shoulder manager. Having someone like McGeeney in the background testing fellas made for a good combination. McGeeney would be less inclined to say, 'I need you do a bit more' but rather 'You think that's training hard? This is training hard.' But he'd also be constructive, telling you to make a small change or two to get more out of your sessions. He had that Roy Keane, Paul O'Connell intensity, and it was a boost to us to have that mindset in the camp.

Great hands: Ronan

I know it's a cliché, but you'll hear it anywhere Gaelic games are discussed. I've often heard lads say it with a straight face. 'You think your man is good, you should see the younger brother – he's twice as good as him.'

With Ronan there was no cliché involved, though. He's always been a fantastic hurler. Some lads mature later than others and don't impress you as kids – they need to grow into their strength or need to improve their touch compared to others. Not Ronan, though. It was clear he was a very good player from the start. It's a(nother) GAA cliché that you can tell who the good players are because they're in central positions all the way up, and that was the case with Ronan.

When I watched him coming up through the grades, under-12, 14, 16, he was always lined up in the middle. With young lads that's where the strongest players are, and Ronan was always playing full-back, centre-back, midfield. And by the time he got to under-16, you could definitely see that he had great potential. A lot of people around the club would say, growing up, that Ronan's playing style was very much like my own father's. I can remember my father playing but not in great detail – the older lads in the club say they were both left-sided with their right hand on top, both kind of wiry in the way they went about their game. But, yeah, Ronan and myself were both kind of playing the same positions really: full-back, centre-back, wing-back.

He has a slightly unusual style, that right hand on top but playing off his left. Unlike me, though, I don't think any coach ever tried to change his style, because he's right-handed. It wouldn't have made any sense to do so anyway, given how well he strikes the ball. He just naturally has better hands than me – way better hands than me. I had to work harder at my hurling than he did, it comes far more naturally to him.

Take his striking, which is fantastic. He has such a sweet strike, left and right. Even in his line-balls and frees, he makes such good contact every time. I think if there was a penalty to be taken, he'd be the only one on the list, both for Tipperary and Sarsfields. We'd even see it when he's playing golf. He has a natural strike for the ball, and when he hits it, he creams it. (Is he a better golfer than me? He is at the moment, but give me time – now I've retired I have more time to work on my game and catch up.)

People asked me over the years whether it was awkward to have him playing in the same area of the field as me – around the half-backs. It's not awkward at all. Why wouldn't you want to have your own brother on a team with you? In every sport, but particularly the GAA, brothers and cousins make up teams all the time. With Ronan, for me the only question was when would he break on to the Tipperary senior team. And that was on merit, certainly, and not because he was my brother.

His progress was smooth enough. He went in first to the Tipperary minors and was playing corner-back when they won the All-Ireland minor in 2012 after a replay. He was still underage for minor the next year, and he was the Tipperary centre-back, which tells you all about his quality. Funnily enough, he never really came to me looking for advice. I'd have given him a couple of pointers here and there, but I wouldn't have overloaded him, particularly when he was getting on fine himself.

And the fact that he was just a better natural hurler than me anyway meant it was more about leaving him off than overdoing the advice.

He probably learned more by watching me at home, in fact, what I'd be doing as regards preparation. He would have seen me, when I was still living at home, arguing with the mother over different foods, for example asking her to buy me fresh fish instead of having crispy baked fish for dinner. So Ronan would have known the level you need to reach for senior inter-county in terms of preparation. He'd have seen me doing my stretches before games, ice baths, calling to Mick Clohessy for the rubs, or staying at home the day before a big match to rest. Because of that, he had an idea of what was required before he even came into the senior set-up with Tipp. He knew those things before the management had to tell him, which probably helped in his development as a player. Because I lived at home till I was in my late twenties, he would have seen that preparation first hand. And as he broke onto the senior team, we did everything together when it came to training, gym work, all of that. We had a routine when it came to big games

– we always used to meet one or two of the lads the day before and go stretching, then head out for a coffee. Over the years it served us well.

Ronan is probably more outgoing than me. People who know me would probably say I can be a bit introverted, put it that way: he's a bit bubblier. Which isn't to say he's a pushover. When you're the older brother there's a presumption that you're there to look after the younger lad, particularly if there's a row in a game. That's not how it is with Ronan, though. He could always stand up for himself. If you watched him over the years you'd see that there weren't too many players who went near him very much. Because they knew by him – he'd just give a little snip, and he'd look at them and say, 'What are you doing?'

I certainly don't remember lads going at him. In 2016, when we played Cork in Thurles, he was centre-back and I was wing-back. We were winning well in the second half, and I can't remember who it was, but one or two of the Cork lads had gone in at him with a bit of pushing and shoving. I recall being on hand and just grabbing the two of them – we have a photo of it at home. Ronan's there, and I'm just standing between the two Cork lads, and the two of us are just looking at the two boys. A bit of a stand-off, but it wasn't a case of me minding him, certainly. He's not the kind of player to take any nonsense, he'd do it fair and square and take you on.

I obviously have huge admiration for what he's done in his career, and seeing him as captain of Tipperary is fantastic. It's a great honour for the whole family, and for him in particular, and shows how strong a character he is. I was 13 or 14 when my father left home, so I had an idea what was going on. These things happen regularly in families, unfortunately. But Ronan was only six or seven, so he didn't really understand, and it would have been tough on him for the few years after. Our father used to come home every so often for a few days and would spend a bit of time with him, but he'd obviously have to go back to Wales, where he was working and living, and Ronan used to get upset every time he'd leave.

It was tough for him, but I think he came out of it stronger, and it made him a better person, a more robust character. It's a situation that's a lot more common now, but it was challenging for him then. I was obviously gutted myself at the time, but I was starting to grow up a bit, and I understood the whole thing. And it happened that I knew other families or had been in school with lads who'd had similar experiences, so I would have spoken to them about it. But because Ronan was only a child, he didn't understand it fully. I always admire him for that, because he just took it and went with it.

Ronan is a handy man to have around the place, which not everybody knows. His hurley-making is another example of how good his hands are. He's got a great work ethic and brilliant hands: put them together and you've got those beautiful hurleys. I often meet lads raving about a hurley he made for them or one they borrowed from a pal. What I don't want to tell them is that it's a skill he picked up from just messing around in the shed. He's just very good to turn his hand to something like that. When my cousin Patrick was building a house Ronan fell in with him and was able to do a lot of the timber work, even though he's not trained as a carpenter.

He put in all the wooden floors in my house. Again, no training or background in it. He just has it. If that were left to me, I'd be fooling and messing for months, doing all the wrong cutting and showing all and sundry I didn't have a clue. Whereas with him, he can just see it. 'That's how it's done.' And he does it.

He came on the panel in 2014, but he had a tough baptism, put it that way, against Galway in the All-Ireland qualifiers that year. He started the game at midfield and came off at half-time, and that was it. He didn't get a chance for the rest of the year, but he started at wing-back in 2015. Since then, he's been a key part of the team. He won his first Munster senior hurling medal in Thurles that year, though we lost the All-Ireland semi-final later on to Galway. The following year we won All-Ireland medals and both of us got All-Stars. The All-Stars are great, but winning the All-Ireland with your brother … I remember meeting my mother there as well, and it was very emotional, the three of us being there together. That win in 2016 is really special. When we won in 2019 it was great as well – you'd never win enough – but we'd done it already in 2016.

Having to retire so abruptly is disappointing, for a number of reasons, but not being able to play for a Tipperary team captained by your own brother is a big one. I'd have given anything to play for him and try to help the team succeed. My form was good at the club last year so I was ready to go for another year at least, and I had an inkling that Ronan would have been in the running for captain for 2022.

It was gas. Before I left the team WhatsApp group, the management had the poll up for the players to pick who they thought the captain or vice-captain should be. It was a couple of days before I'd decided to make my announcement, so I got my vote in. Needless to say, I voted for Ronan. (Fair enough, call a stewards' inquiry if you like.)

I'd been disappointed when I was captain in 2017 and

2018. We were close in 2017, beaten by Galway by a point in the All-Ireland semi-final, but in 2018, we didn't perform. We lost out in the last group game of the Munster championship, so my time as captain wasn't that successful. I didn't want the same thing to happen to Ronan, but unfortunately it did in the first year. I'm just hoping he won't be remembered for that.

As was the case with the hurling, he wouldn't have sat me down and asked me a load of questions about becoming a garda. He would have seen what I did in Templemore, what I went through, and then for a few years after. And I suppose he was looking at it and thinking, *Yeah, that would be interesting*. He saw that I was getting on fine at it, and that it suited me. He'd done arts in college, so he was probably at a crossroads and eventually decided, *Feck it, I'll go for it*.

Our cousin Dennis and himself went in at the same time, which probably helped Ronan a bit. Though as I've said already, anyone who knows him will know he's his own man.

More than a game

On a parallel track to our rivalry with Kilkenny, we fell into a trilogy of great games against Galway. All at the All-Ireland semi-final stage. All close games that went down to the wire. All of them won by a point.

As a kid in Thurles, Galway wouldn't have been on my radar the way they'd have figured for some of the lads up in north Tipperary. As I got older and met them in minor finals, that changed a little, and we beat them in an under-21 All-Ireland final as well, but at underage level you don't have long-running rivalries. It's not about 'They beat us last year so we'll get them this year,' because of the turnover of players from one year to the next. The one difference when we were playing minor was Joe Canning, who was a very well-known player even then, but for the most part – like all minors – I wouldn't have known their underage teams inside out.

I was aware of their history as a great hurling county, and we beat them in 2010 in the All-Ireland qualifiers, but a pointer towards the future was visible that year at under-21 level. When we played them in the final we won well, carrying great momentum from the senior final a few days before. The fact that the game was on in Semple Stadium didn't hurt either. I got to captain the team to an All-Ireland title 200 metres from my own club: the stuff dreams are made of. We were riding the crest of a wave at that point, full of confidence, not even training that much but going from game to game. It was no surprise that we ended up brushing Galway aside that particular evening, but they had serious players on that team: David Burke, Davy Glennon, Johnny Coen. Plenty of lads we'd see again at senior level.

In 2015 there was a shadow over the Tipperary team with the news of Noel McGrath's illness. We went on a training camp around March – out to Alicante, the usual spot – and got the heads down, working away. Noel didn't train, he stayed in his room and we just thought he was under the weather with a bug. I'd be very friendly with Noel, having come up all the way from minor with him, and I recall going up to the room one day, the two of us lying back in our beds chatting or picking through the phones. He didn't do anything for that week, though, and when we came back we all went our separate ways as usual.

A few days later I was at a funeral – a member of the Thurles Sarsfields club – and I got a call from my mother.

'Did you hear anything about Noel?'

I said no, and she told me that he had cancer – she had heard from a mutual acquaintance – and I was in shock. At that stage he was 25 and probably felt invincible. Like every 25-year-old, myself included, particularly when you're playing inter-county hurling. I texted him to ask if it was true and he texted back: it was. I met up with him soon enough after that and he told me the story, how he'd discovered it. That was a fair jolt, to see someone you soldiered with in All-Ireland finals and in league games on rainy afternoons getting a knock like that.

But he came back in as the summer wore on and was part of the panel for the semi-final against Galway. It was a huge lift for us to have him around the place at training, never mind what he might have contributed on the field of play. It wasn't something that was discussed in detail in the group. When it became public knowledge, early in the year, we were still involved in the National League and facing into a knock-out game in Nowlan Park.

For a change of scenery as much as anything else, Eamon had suggested a training session in Nowlan Park, and Noel came down for that. It was our first sight of him really since the news had broken, and he spoke to the group very well that night. He said he was going to face this thing head-on and we were to concentrate on the job we had to do ourselves – it was a speech that hit home with everyone and lifted us all for the season ahead.

When we made the All-Ireland semi-final that year we knew what to expect from Galway. I'm not sure they knew what to expect from one of our key players, though. Séamus Callanan had been good the previous year and he carried that form into 2015; there was a huge change in him from the 2014 season on, really. In any of the games he played at that time it was clear that his confidence was high. He was more of a team player than ever before, recognising that it was important to make the players around him look good as well as impressing himself.

By 2015 the likes of Eoin Kelly and John O'Brien,

experienced leaders in the forward line, had gone, and Larry was clearly coming towards the end of his own career, so we needed forwards to stand up. Séamus took that on, and it suited him. He had been in and around the senior panel from 2008, when he burst on the scene, so he wasn't inexperienced himself. He'd been in and out of the team but there was no doubting the talent – it was just a matter of getting it out of him.

Eamon was a massive part of that, helping Séamus to develop as a player, getting him to realise there was more to the game than simply getting your name on the scoresheet. Séamus became more of a leader from 2014 on, and 2015 was a good example of that. In training he was very impressive and I was confident he'd cut loose against Galway, his form had been so good. That's the benefit a team can get from a really good manager. Eamon loved forward play and getting the most out of forwards, improving their movement and team play, and Séamus reaped the rewards of his coaching and management in those seasons.

In the Munster final against Waterford earlier that summer I'd busted up the AC joint in my left arm when I ran into 'Brick' Walsh. But I was in luck. Waterford were playing an out-and-out sweeper on their side, and I was told to do the same on ours; only for that I wouldn't have been able to play, because physically I wouldn't have been able to mark a man. In that Munster final I was going for the ball, and when I won it I was looking for someone to hand-pass it to immediately. I couldn't strike the ball.

On *The Sunday Game* that night, Eddie Brennan was singing my praises as he analysed one passage of play. 'Look at this defending from Paudie Maher,' he was saying. 'He knew he couldn't reach the ball with the hurley in his left hand so he switches the hurley to his right.' I'd blocked Maurice Shanahan in that passage of play and had given the ball off, but it wasn't clever defending from me – I couldn't raise the hurley in my left hand because of the AC joint, so I used my right and got the hurley in the way of the ball.

I was lucky that there was a five-week gap between the Munster final and the All-Ireland semi-final. I barely trained in that period as I was trying to rehab the shoulder, and I was conscious of that going into the game. I was physically fit but I hadn't done as much hurling as I would have liked, and I wasn't quite as sharp as I would have wanted for a game that big.

For that Galway game I was centre-back and picked

up Cyril Donnellan, who was a strong, direct player. Joe Canning would float around to different positions and Conor Whelan, a newcomer, stayed inside in the full-forward line, but Donnellan was a traditional centre-forward – bustling, stand underneath the dropping ball and fight for possession. Joe was the danger man but we wouldn't have had elaborate plans to tie him down. My impression was that he tended to have a pattern to his movements – he'd either be in full-forward or drifting around wing-forward. He didn't get stuck inside in the corner and he tended to stay out of the centre-forward zone, so in terms of positions he favoured 14 or 12.

We had James Barry at full-back and he wasn't going to track Joe all around the field, so whoever was out on the wing would pick him up if he was out there, and James would mark him if he drifted back in around the square. It can be that straightforward sometimes. I know that hurling is more analysed now than ever, and both players and coaches have to be more tactically aware, but there's also the instinctive part of the game.

Eamon was very good to discuss that aspect. He'd stress the need to be aware of the team's structure, but he'd also point out the need to play what was happening in front of you, and to trust your instincts in those circumstances. You might have a plan for particular players, whether to man-mark them or to rely on the players in different positions marking them if they popped up in those positions, but you still have to go for the ball yourself and trust yourself. You can see a touch of that in how Limerick play even if someone like Tony Kelly is on the other side – Limerick will trust their own plan and play to that, believing that'll overcome his contributions to the Clare cause.

If I were involved with a team that's a point I'd be making – for all the talk about structures, you must be able to deal with particular circumstances. No matter how aware you are of the game plan, if you find yourself in a particular part of the field then you have to play the hand that you've been dealt. Eamon and Liam would have been very strong on dealing with those situations as they arose: 'If you find yourself there, so what? Go for it.'

Séamus went for it, certainly. He ended up with 3–9 and he was on fire, to put it mildly. He got a goal early on to settle us but Galway hung in there. Over the course of the game they got no goal but hit 26 points, which is good scoring. Séamus got goals at the right times in the second half, but whenever we got those goals they hit back with points and we didn't get the benefit of those scores, if you like.

And then Noel came in as a sub with about eight minutes to go. In fairness, the reception he got from all the supporters in Croke Park, Tipperary and Galway, was unreal. It might have been a tight match with a place in the All-Ireland final at stake but people recognised what he'd been through, the treatment regime he'd taken on, and they showed their appreciation. It nearly became the ultimate fairy tale late on in the game, when he snapped over a point at the canal end, but Jason Flynn got an equaliser as the clock hit 70 minutes.

The game becomes a bit different then. Every player is well aware that they have the winning of the game in their hands – and the losing of it. A hand on someone's back could give away the free that loses the match, and that bit of fear can get into your head. You're glancing up at the clock and you see 71 minutes … 72 minutes. (In the Tipperary county final in 2021 the ultimate nightmare happened to me – the game was level in injury time when I went out to tackle John McGrath in the corner. I got my hand caught in underneath him and gave away a free, and he popped that over for the winner. Last puck of the game. My last play in hurling!)

You can't help that kind of thought coming into your head, though. *I don't want to be the one who makes the mistake*, or even *Don't hit the ball down this wing to me*. When it's level like that you'd be half-hoping the referee would just blow it up to have another day out. The other thing to consider is that at that point in the game, the whole thing is chaos anyway. Fellas have gone off, fellas have come in as subs, some lad is cramping up, another lad is gone in corner-forward for a rest after a long run, nobody knows who's marking who once it gets to 72, 73 minutes. That's something people who stress structure and tactics tend to forget. The structure may hold for 50 minutes or more, but at a certain point positions cease to have any real meaning, and players end up grabbing whoever is closest to them whenever the ball comes near. Any plans that have been rehearsed in training are gone out the window.

At that point it's just about trying to win the ball, and credit to Galway, they won it at just the right time. Joe popped up in the middle of the field and had plenty of time to look around and pick out a pass, which was exactly what you didn't want to see as a defender. Shane Moloney had come on as a sub for Galway and I was sitting back to screen the full-back line. I had an eye on him but I wasn't touch-tight: as soon as Joe hit the ball I knew I hadn't a hope of getting close enough to put in a tackle on Shane. If I'd flung myself full-length I wouldn't have cut the pass out. In desperation, I flicked my hurley across to try and hook him, even if it had somehow stopped the shot there would have been a free, but at that stage it was desperation stakes. He put it over and that was it.

The way we lost the game was a disaster, obviously. A point. A whole year is gone in an hour and a quarter's play, and you're inconsolable. But we only had to look over to one corner of the dressing room to put the whole thing in context. Losing a game wasn't a disaster. Getting sick was far worse. But Noel faced it down and got over it. And having him back in the group more than made up for losing a match.

Eamon was emotional enough afterwards. He's an emotional guy anyway, and Tipperary games brought that emotion to the fore. He probably felt something was coming with the team, and for it to get away from us at the end was devastating for him. And for us. He was one manager we were mad to win an All-Ireland for, because we felt he deserved it. He lives in Galway so there was an extra layer to that game anyway, but we were desperate to get to a final again to win it for him. We knew Mick Ryan was due to take over from him and we had great time for Mick, but it was a huge regret not to win an All-Ireland for Eamon.

Meeting Joe, deleting Twitter and an All-Ireland medal

When Eamon was manager he had Micheál Donoghue as part of the backroom team. He had been giving us insights into Galway ahead of the All-Ireland semi-final in 2015 – I remember him ringing me a couple of times to discuss the players I'd likely end up marking in that game – but when Eamon stepped down Micheál went as well. At first there were suggestions he might stay with us, but then the Galway vacancy opened up and he duly popped up as Galway manager in 2016.

It was no surprise. Even from the work he'd done with us in the background it was clear how good he'd be as a manager, that he'd be someone players would want to play for, and the pull of his own county was obviously something he wouldn't turn down. But it was strange to have someone managing against you when they'd been part of your own team's backroom just a year beforehand.

We had a new manager, of course. After Eamon's years with the forwards, we had a lot of backs in the backroom all of a sudden – Mick Ryan was a back, he had Declan Fanning in as a coach (another back) along with John Madden (another back). Conor Stakelum was the only forward connection, which made a change, though we still had Gary and Lukasz on the fitness side, and we trained hard again that winter.

Mick was a real manager in the sense that he was overseeing what was going on as opposed to doing a lot of the sessions himself. His management style wasn't too different to his playing style – tough, direct, hardy. He'd give it to you straight with no messing around: 'I want more from you,' or 'Do it this way.' Everyone played for him and there was no issue with his approach, though it might have helped that the group was more mature at that stage. Ronan was one of the younger lads, Séamus Kennedy and John McGrath were new enough, but a lot of the rest of us were experienced. Some of us had been in an All-Ireland final seven years earlier, so we'd been around the block.

People have often asked me, 'What did ye do differently in 2016 that made the team successful compared to other years?' The truth is there wasn't a huge amount that was different. Early on that year the league wasn't too hectic at all – Clare beat us in a quarter-final and our performances were average enough. Again, with perspective, you'd say we weren't miles away in 2015 if we'd only lost an All-Ireland semi-final by a point in injury time, but we also benefited in 2016 from all the hard work we'd done the previous few years, and all the experience we'd gathered in those seasons.

Good performances early on in the championship helped, though. We had a good win over Cork in Munster in May and had a better win over Limerick a month afterwards, in many ways. 'Bubbles' got a red card after about 20 minutes against Limerick but we still won handily. They got a late consolation goal which gave the scoreboard a better look, but we took a lot of confidence from winning a big championship game with 14 men.

Mick had us firing well, and to give him credit, because he'd known 12 months in advance that he'd be taking over, he'd clearly been watching closely what we'd done with Eamon and had built on that. He didn't try to reinvent the wheel but he did make some positional changes at the start of the year and kept the team settled throughout the season. For instance, I'd been floating between 6 and 7, Brendan Maher had been centre-forward for a while but had also played midfield and half-back, so there were a few of us never entirely sure where we'd be. Under Mick, though, Séamus Kennedy was 5, Ronan was 6, I was 7, Brendan was 8, Mikey Breen was 9 ... it was as though he had that in mind coming in from the start, that that was where we'd play, and by sticking to that, the team was settled.

We all knew what we were doing in every game rather than taking the opposition into account and changing everything to deal with them. Instead of thinking, *We're playing Cork so you follow him and you follow him*, he brought an attitude of 'We'll play the way we play, lads and whoever we play, we play.' That gave players confidence, myself included. There had been times with Tipperary when I'd feel I was playing well, but that didn't mean I was 100 per cent certain where on the team I'd be playing on a particular day. That isn't ideal. Even allowing for the fact that you have to adapt depending on the game or the opposition, players like certainty.

I'd say 2016 was one of my best years with Tipperary, and a lot of that came from knowing exactly where I'd be playing, so I knew my job every day. Declan Fanning was a huge part of that too. Eamon had brought him on board with Tipperary as a second coach in 2015 to show him the ropes, and that was a help because he hit the ground running. In 2015 he'd run a few drills but the following year he was the main coach, and because he was a breath of fresh air, that energised the whole thing all over again.

Some of us had played with him but all of us admired him for what he'd done for Tipperary over the years, so he got a great response from the players. When I joined the panel in 2009 he was one of the leaders on the team, and when he became coach I wasn't going to leave a stone unturned in my preparation. You could say the approach that year was direct, uncomplicated, settled, and players really hit form. If I had to pick out one crucial factor it was probably the settled team. In subsequent years we weren't as effective, and it wasn't an accident there was uncertainty sometimes about where lads were playing, but 2016 was the perfect illustration of that settled approach.

We won the Munster title relatively easily and got back to face Galway again in the All-Ireland semi-final. Despite what people might think, I wouldn't overstate the 'they beat us last year so we're going to have our revenge this year'. That wouldn't have been our attitude. We'd have focused on Micheál Donoghue but not because he'd been in our camp the previous season; more that we expected him to come up with a different challenge for us. We had our own man driving us on anyway. Mick Ryan was passionate about Tipperary hurling and had us tuned in long before that game was played, but he ramped it up the day of the game. At that time, before games we'd usually go to the Gibson Hotel down near the 3Arena because it was close to Croke Park, and that day he brought us into a huddle before leaving for the stadium and said a few words. He spoke about the jersey and standing up for it and fighting for it – getting onto the bus I can remember thinking, *We won't be beaten here today.*

The game itself was a good one. Conor Cooney got a goal for them early on but we were going well: we weren't panicked and we stayed in touch. There was a great pace to the game throughout and a couple of the incidents probably stayed in people's memories long after the final whistle. About 20 minutes in, I was holding my position but drifting slightly to the left when David Burke won the ball in their half, came out with it and flicked it across to Joe Canning, right out on the wing. He took the ball but he had to get past Noel McGrath, so I started making my way in that direction because I could see he'd try to break Noel's tackle, and as he did I could see that the challenge was on and I went to meet him.

It was one of those things that if you're an inch off with the challenge it's probably a red card and you're gone, but I timed it just right and caught him on the sideline. I knew it was a serious challenge – I was split myself when it happened, probably from the face mask, and had to go off for a few minutes with a blood injury from the collision, but people forget that Joe stayed on afterwards. He got attention down on the sideline, but he came back into the game after a few minutes.

Later in the half he pulled a hamstring running out towards the middle of the field and was substituted. So he didn't have to go off because of running in to me. People spoke about it a lot at the time, and since, but the best way I could put it was that that was a compliment to Joe. The kind of player he was, when I saw him breaking free I had to go to him to put in a challenge. Another Galway player in the same situation and I mightn't even have left my position, but because it was him I knew it was an opportunity to make a statement. If it was done now there might be cards involved, though I knew as soon as we collided that I'd caught him flush on the shoulder. I knew instinctively there'd be no issue with a free or a yellow card, though I didn't know I was bleeding myself until Dr Brendan Murphy, our medic, started roaring at me to come off the field for stitches.

With a few minutes to go before the break Galway were getting on top, and Joseph Cooney played a fantastic pass across the face of the goal to Conor Cooney. It was one of those passes that when you see it coming across, as a defender you're thinking, *Trouble here*. As a half-back your instinct should always be, when the ball is played into the corner as it was then, to sprint back to offer some cover. There were numbers being drawn towards the ball, which made Joseph's pass all the more dangerous for us.

But even as he got his head up to see what was on, I got it in my head that I had a chance to get back. I felt it in my stomach, almost: *I've a chance here*. I sprinted as hard as I could and when Conor wound up I knew I'd get the hook in. My hurley caught his but I still had to dive full-length to do it. I started sliding past and my only thought was that I'd slide all the way past the ball and he'd get a chance to pull on it, but in fairness to the lads they got bodies around it straightaway.

It can happen in a game – even as the ball was about to come across I got a sense I had a chance to get to him: the thought just flashed through my head, *This is on for me*. To give him his due, I didn't think he had too much of a wind-up striking the ball, either.

It was a turning point alright. If they'd scored a goal it would have been 2–9 to 0–10 with half-time approaching, so stopping the goal lifted the team. It lifted me too – I got a lot of confidence from that. We brought 'Bubbles' on and he made a difference straightaway. People don't appreciate the sheer talent someone like him has. In training, to see some of the things he'd do … you might be pucking around, say, and he'd switch hands and hurl away with his left hand on top instead of his right. And nearly put me to shame with his flicks and tricks, even though I've hurled left hand on top all my life.

He's just naturally talented – football, soccer, golf, whatever he takes up he can do – and it's just a matter of getting it out of him consistently. Any of the years he was going well for Tipperary he nearly won games on his own, hitting points at his ease. His striking is so good that he'd often get the ball in a position on the field that if it was anyone else there you'd be roaring at them to work it out to someone in a better position, but because 'Bubbles' had it you always knew there was a fair chance he'd put it over. Having been sent off against Limerick earlier in the year he probably felt he had a point to prove, and the goal he got certainly did that. Mick Ryan would probably have felt he'd have to earn his place rather than just sail back in, and having someone come off the bench hungry and eager to prove a point is always a plus.

It was a goal only he could have scored, really. They were a point or two ahead when John McGrath got the ball and turned his man before passing it in to 'Bubbles', but he had no angle, he was almost on the end line. Almost any forward would have wound up and tried to blast it in over the keeper's head into the roof of the net with pure power, but not 'Bubbles'. His hurling brain is so acute that he saw immediately he had another option, and he slapped it down and in on the keeper's near side: goal. (He did the same in the All-Ireland final, of course. He got the ball, soloed through, and I've no doubt he was thinking, *Where would the goalkeeper not want this shot to go?* – and then put it right there.) We needed John McGrath to get another goal after a fantastic pass by Séamie Callanan and that put us on the right road. It didn't have as dramatic an end as the previous year's semi-final, but it was a huge win for us.

I can remember dancing around the pitch with Mickey Cahill at the final whistle because winning such a tight game meant so much, particularly after losing such a tight game the year before to the same opposition. Out on the field there wasn't a sense of *We have it won now, the All-Ireland is ours*. We had to play Kilkenny in the final and we hadn't won an All-Ireland in six years, but that didn't stop the feeling of relief at the final whistle. We probably celebrated that semi-final win more than any others because we recognised at some level that it was worth more than most. We needed it, and we did it.

There was no talk about the challenge on Joe afterwards within the group. Nobody said, 'That was some hit,' or anything, but when I turned on the phone I saw clips of it on social media. It was around that time that social media was beginning to be an issue for players, I think. I was on social media myself and following everything and anything, and it didn't bother me. If someone posted something about me I'd have read it but it never affected me. As time wore on I noticed that people were becoming far more critical, though. The smallest thing and you'd be slated. A bad performance and you'd be slaughtered; if the man you were marking got through for a goal there'd be a torrent of abuse about you. After the incident with Michael Rice against Kilkenny a couple of years before I got plenty of abuse and a lot of that came from social media accounts based in Kilkenny, or which seemed to be based there.

Around 2016, I decided to delete Twitter and those social media accounts. It just wasn't worth it anymore – the odd time some person paid you a compliment was drowned out by people abusing you up and down. If you gave a man-of-the-match performance they were still slating you, and I decided it wasn't worth the grief. I remember thinking these were lads who'd never hurled at all, or who'd never been involved in high-performance sport, but that didn't mean the abuse was any easier to take.

I'd be interested in all sports – in soccer, rugby, golf, all of them – and Twitter was always handy just to check out what was going on in various competitions, and I eventually opened an account to keep an eye on sport but didn't open it to the public, so I could pick and choose what I followed and who followed me. As I got older I became less interested in what people thought about me, but you could still be surprised by the online reaction to something that happened on the field. In 2019 we played Laois in the qualifiers in Croke Park, and out on the sideline one of the Laois lads swung and hit me, right across the knee. When you get a belt right on the kneecap like that your leg goes dead, and I went down in a heap. (I met a pal of mine a couple of days after the game and he said he could hear the hurley hit my knee from where he was sitting in the stand: a fair belt.)

I was holding my knee, in agony, and the Laois lad got sent off. Afterwards we were having some grub and Eddie Brennan came over to me. He was managing Laois at the time and I knew him well through the Garda College, and we were chatting away.

'You'd better not turn on your Twitter account tonight,' he said to me.

And of course the first thing I did was have a look, and there were lads giving out about me throwing myself down on the ground to get someone sent off: complete nonsense. I couldn't help but think what the reaction would have been if I'd been the one sent off. I'm sure there wouldn't have been that much sympathy, but then again, that's social media. You just can't win.

Claire

The big change in my life came in 2017. As part of my garda community work I had a group of kids from a school in Limerick come down to the Garda College in Templemore for a school tour, and there was a female garda, who immediately grabbed my attention, with a group of school kids from Kildare, where she was based. We crossed paths in the college's museum.

And they say romance is dead.

That was Claire. Since then she's said I made the first overtures, and I've said she was the one who made the first move. I'd be inclined to give the credit to a mutual friend who engineered the introduction (but Claire still says she has the text messages to prove her case).

She's a Clare woman – her family live outside Ennis but the family are Newmarket-on-Fergus on her mother's side while her father is north Clare. They're mad GAA people, so we all have that in common. Obviously they're followers of Clare in hurling and football but to be fair to her, if Tipperary weren't playing Clare she and her family would support me, they're very encouraging. In 2019 she put on a Tipp t-shirt for the All-Ireland final, which was a fair declaration. (Not as much when Clare and Tipp were playing, though: their official line on those occasions would be, 'Best of luck, hope you play well but that we win.')

Her support is very important to me. In 2018 I was captain of Tipperary but the year didn't go too well, and I would have taken that very badly. She was very encouraging at that time, which I really appreciated, motivating me to go again and to come back stronger. When I got the news about my neck she was the one who made sure I consulted widely, that I covered all the avenues before making a final decision.

Claire is like a lot of us – with her own family and friends she's chatty, but reserved enough with strangers. A bit like myself, and we're probably more alike than different: it's certainly not a case of opposites attracting. She's a strong-minded person. She has her views on how things should be done, but she's open to suggestion as well. For instance, when I got to a stage where I wanted to buy my own place, I was keen to have somewhere in Thurles or nearabouts. I was hurling and everything was focused on the area around Thurles, but she's from Ennis, so ...

When we thought about somewhere to live we considered Nenagh as a possibility as a halfway location. But it was pointed out that we knew nobody in Nenagh, or Limerick, and that if we bought a house in Thurles we'd have my family as support. Claire saw the sense in that. (Though I hear the odd comment about us going to live in Ennis at some point. To be discussed in the future.)

In fairness, she upped sticks and moved over to this side of the country. Between hurling and later, the coffee shop, she saw I had a lot going on here and was willing to make that move. She works for a software development company, ACMS, in Limerick. While still a garda she decided to do a course part-time and when a job came up in that field in Limerick, she went for it.

I have great admiration for her and for her strength. She'd turn her hand to anything and would take any challenge head on and do well. She's very determined. For instance, she enrolled on a strength and conditioning course with Setanta College recently, and I was saying, 'You'll pass that no bother.' But she told me she wants an A grade, not to just get over the line. That's her mentality.

Like anyone who's involved with an inter-county player, she might sound off the odd time about the calendar and the demands of the game. And like anyone who's on an inter-county panel, I had to be selfish over the years when it came to preparation. Everything revolved around my routine when it came to holidays, weekends away, weddings of friends, all those aspects of the social life. And because I took my commitments with the Sarsfields as seriously as I did with Tipperary, there wasn't much let-up when the county season ended, so we missed out on a fair amount of social opportunities over the years.

In all honesty I have so much admiration for Claire and the way she treats people, the way she looks after her family, how thoughtful and caring she is, the way she looks after me (and our dog Pookie, of course, the boss of the house). I'm so lucky to have stumbled upon her that day in Templemore, I love her so much and I'm looking forward to making up for all the sacrifices she's made for me over the years.

One point

The difference between seasons can be huge. In 2016 I never really felt like the year was going to get away from us. We were consistent all the way through. In 2017 that feeling wasn't there. As a season it reminded me more of 2015 in that we weren't as sure about how things were going.

It was my first year as captain, though. Silver linings. Mick rang me early in 2017 and said Brendan had done his stint as captain. I'd been vice-captain and Mick said I was the new captain, to keep on doing what I'd been doing all along. It wasn't something I was ever fixated on, but it was still a huge privilege and honour to captain Tipperary. From my experience as captain, winning an under-21 All-Ireland and winning county and Munster titles with the club, I felt captaincy brought the best out of me, having that extra responsibility.

It wasn't a big pressure for me. I was probably playing the best hurling of my career in those years so the confidence was high – I'd won a couple of All-Stars and had All-Ireland medals. Captain of Tipperary? Fantastic. There were challenges along the way, though. That was the year Mick dropped Cathal Barrett from the panel. Cathal played in the first game, against Cork, and picked up an injury, but Mick cut him from the panel for disciplinary reasons anyway. I remember Mick saying, 'We've no choice, Paudie, and that's it.' I wasn't going to say, 'Hang on a second, let's discuss it.' The management team were in agreement with Mick's decision, and it was a decision – he told me for information, not for consultation.

I can remember thinking, *Why's this happening on my watch?*, but it was never a situation where you'd go to management and say, 'Look, bring him back for this one match.' If you did that, you'd be going against everything that a team or a panel is supposed to be about. But there's no doubt he was a loss. A fully healthy Cathal Barrett might have made the difference in a one-point defeat, which was how we exited the championship, but Mick had his rules and standards, and if those weren't met then there were consequences. We accepted that.

It wasn't easy when we got beaten early on by Cork, and I couldn't help but compare it to the previous year, when the whole thing ran like clockwork. You can't help thinking, *Is this happening because I'm captain? Is that why fellas are taking the foot off the pedal a bit? Is it something I'm doing wrong?* But when I took a step back and had a good look at my own preparation and performances, I was happy enough that I was leading by example.

I was doing what I'd always done, getting myself ready to the best of my ability and leading the team as well as I could, and once I realised that, I was happy I was doing justice to the role.

In 2017 I was the only Tipperary player to win an All-Star, which bore out my belief that I was playing well. But it was still disappointing not to have won some silverware as captain. I wouldn't have too many fond memories of the captaincy but at least I could say in honesty that my own standards didn't drop. And of course, if we'd beaten Galway by a point in the famous semi-final, instead of losing by a point, it would have been all forgotten anyway.

Joe's point is the part of the game that people remember, obviously enough, but there were plenty of other sideshows that day. Micheál Donoghue was in his second year over Galway so he was more experienced as a manager, but I had enough to deal with to be too concerned with our former adviser. I got repaid with interest for the hit on Joe Canning that day in Croke Park too – I went out to take Gearóid McInerney but he saw me coming and rocked me back with a good shot. The crowd loved it, of course, and I nearly laughed myself: *That one was coming for a while*, I was thinking. At least I was able to play on, but it was a tough, physical challenge. They were very strong at that stage. I would have been marking Cathal Mannion because of this narrative of putting me on a runner to test my legs, but even he was six foot one, not a small, fast lad.

Galway had plenty of size to contend with. Joe Canning, Jonathan Glynn, they're big. Conor Whelan is nearly six foot and powerful. The Cooneys, Aidan Harte, they're all big men.

Joe was the key man. He hit the winner, but he was good in other parts of that game as well. He was always cute enough to stay on the move and to make it hard for the opposition to tie him down, and that day he drifted out to the middle of the field. When the game started to break up late on he picked up ball there – he'd got one point from long range before that one.

In injury time he lined up that long-range free to try to win it, but he was well back in his own half. I remember thinking it was a huge ask even for a player of his calibre. It dropped short and squeezed through but Darren Gleeson stopped it and we cleared it out to the wing, away from danger. Looking back, should we have worked it out the field? It's easy to say now that that was an option, but in the moment it's just a matter of getting it out of the danger area – anywhere will do, nearly.

It probably worked well for them that, because Joe had taken that free, he was able to motor up the right wing almost unmarked, because all eyes were on the ball and what was going to happen inside in the square. Credit to Johnny Coen, he won a great ball out on the wing and had the calmness to turn back to give someone else the shot. And of all the players on the Galway team, with respect, the one man you didn't want to see putting his hand up for Johnny's pass was Joe. The lads did their best to close him down – Niall O'Meara came very close to getting a hurley in the way, but Joe got the shot off. I remember seeing the ball rise, and looking back over my shoulder to track it going between the posts.

Again, people think that was the end of the game, but play resumed and we got one more chance, a sight of goal and an opportunity to level it. From the puckout after Joe's point, the ball broke to 'Bubbles' near the sideline on the Hogan Stand side. He got his shot away, to be fair to him, but it was a snap shot and dropped wide. All over.

Afterwards the sensation was disappointment, but there was also a feeling that we'd left it all out on the field at least. We hadn't started the championship well. Despite being reigning All-Ireland champions Cork had beaten us in Semple Stadium, and we'd had to grind our way back into contention. We beat Dublin in Thurles, and Clare in the new Páirc Uí Chaoimh. That game gave us hope we were back on track, but it was a year of missed opportunities, really.

We felt it was an All-Ireland we might have sneaked, but we couldn't get it done on the day. In hindsight you might think, *Well, it took a great score in a great game to put us out*, but really that's not a consolation.

It's nearly worse, if anything, to come that close to an All-Ireland final. As usual there'd been plenty of negativity in the county after an early championship defeat, plenty of people asking what was wrong with the team, but we got the show back on the road to some extent. That said, the team wasn't as settled as the year before. We were swapping goalkeepers, for instance, which is never a good look for a team – that only settled towards the end of the year, when we got our best team on the field. That was another big contrast with 2016.

Another semi-final. Another point. Another year gone.

2019: if we get to Croke Park, we'll flourish

As usual, the rumour mill kicked in when Mick left. This name and that name were floating around, but eventually I got a text from one of the other players. Sheedy is interested in coming back as manager.

When I got the text I was in the house, and I told Ronan, and clearly he took notice of my excitement at the prospect of Liam coming back. And that excitement was genuine. With him coming back I would have expected the preparation to go to another level again based on his stint a few years before. When it was formally announced, it was clear that the older players were particularly happy. We knew the standards Liam would set, what he'd demand of us but what he'd also be demanding of himself and the management team, his attention to detail, the energy that he'd bring to the role ...

In all honesty, we probably got a bit giddy at the prospect, and it was just what we needed. As an older group of players, relatively speaking, we were all facing into the back end of our careers and needed that boost of energy from somewhere to drive us on in those last few years of playing inter-county. And no one better than Liam to give that.

There weren't huge differences in our relationship with Liam. Obviously there were a lot of changes in our personal situations – we'd all been teenagers fresh out of school, almost, when he'd been manager previously. Now lads were a decade older, some married, responsible, full adults. But the only real difference was that Liam probably saw us as being experienced enough to give more leadership than in 2009 or 2010, when Eoin Kelly and Brendan Cummins were around. Liam still wanted from me what he'd wanted when I was 20, regarding training, preparation, getting in the best shape as possible, and it was the same for the other players of my generation.

A narrative emerged later that he'd been very loyal to us, to that older group of players, but I wouldn't necessarily agree with that. I'd argue that there were good reasons why he stuck with us – we'd set good standards, high standards, we were fit and healthy enough to continue, and for the most part we were performing at the level needed for inter-county. The throwaway comment heard around Tipperary a lot back then was that it was about time Liam blooded a few newer players, but that contradicted one of the oldest ideas in the book, that a team is picked on the basis of what the management sees in training – that that's where you get your chance to win a place in the team for big games. On that basis I felt Liam was picking the best team available to him, because I was at those training sessions and played in those practice games. I don't think it was a case of picking players because of their reputations or because he was close to us.

In any case, only five of us had been there back in 2010. Everybody else apart from myself, Noel McGrath, Bonner Maher, Séamus Callanan and Brendan Maher were, in essence, new players to Liam. So it wasn't as if he was retaining the whole group from ten years previously; the lads who'd come in from around 2012 were as 'new' to him as players who came in around 2019.

Break it down a bit further and you realise Bonner was injured for a good portion of Liam's second management term, so he was really only picking four lads who'd been there in his first term. And those four lads won All-Stars that year, so it's not as if any of us was hanging on by our fingernails. I certainly felt we justified being picked on the team.

(And of course you saw the exact reverse of that thinking a year or two later. I retired in 2022, Brendan Maher retired, Séamus was out with an injury, so you'd expect the whole county would be saying, 'Now we'll bring in the new lads.' Yet for months I couldn't walk down the street in Thurles without lads coming up to me saying, 'We needed ye to hang on for another couple of years, it's a pity ye had to pack it in.' I thought it was funny, but I couldn't help but point out to a couple of them that that made a change from the previous tune: 'Ye were trying non-stop to get us dropped for about three years before that!')

The big difference then was the new round robin format, playing games week in, week out rather than having two weeks or longer between each outing. The previous year, 2018, the first year of the new system, we'd ended up playing our games four weeks in a row, one after another: we'd lost our first game and we were under pressure immediately.

We drew with Cork and drew with Waterford, so we kept ourselves alive into the last weekend, but playing those four weeks in a row was a big ask.

What was noticeable in 2019 was that the system had changed, so every team got a week off somewhere along the line, but the importance of the first game remained. And when Liam came in he built everything in terms of preparation around the first game in the round robin, away to Cork in Páirc Uí Chaoimh. That was the one to nail because we were at home the following week to Waterford, so a win in Cork would have set us up lovely for that game and the rest of the championship. It would give us immediate momentum.

Our run-in wasn't terrific if you were looking in from the outside. Our National League petered out in a loss to Dublin at the quarter-final stage, but Liam's experience really showed then, because he gave the whole set-up a shot of adrenaline. We'd prepared well since the previous November, physically we were flying it, but the buzz of Liam's return had begun to wear off as the league wore on (we were getting used to him) but then he made an announcement after the league ended. He brought a couple of us into a room in the stadium and said, 'Lads, Eamon O'Shea is joining the backroom from next week on.'

We had huge respect for Eamon, he had been there himself as a manager and knew a lot of the players well. Everyone was mad about him, so hearing he was going to fall back in to fine-tune the team in the lead-in to the championship ... immediately the preparations were boosted, everyone knuckled down, and we got focused on Cork. It also shows how shrewd a manager Liam was. Whether he had that lined up all along and was waiting for Eamon's schedule to open up to announce it, or whether he'd been onto Eamon the whole time and finally got him to agree, he wasn't going to say. But there was no point in having Eamon around in December and January for physical training, for instance, when there isn't much opportunity to work on forward play, and Darragh Egan and Tommy Dunne were on hand for coaching. Eamon came in then to re-energise the whole thing, and with so many top-class coaches around we were bound to improve both offensively and defensively. The timing couldn't have been better.

It all came to fruition that day in Páirc Uí Chaoimh. We won by seven points and we were humming. It set us up for the round robin nicely because we had that cushion immediately. Lose the first game and you're scrambling; win it and you're in charge of your own destiny. The win over Limerick in the round robin was another boost. They were All-Ireland champions, they'd beaten us the year before … that said, it was also a funny enough game in that we were both looking at the Munster final a couple of weeks afterwards.

Limerick didn't play Cian Lynch or Declan Hannon that day, though Cian came on in the second half. But it didn't devalue the win for us. We weren't going to let up; we wanted to keep going rather than break our own momentum. That's something people often don't appreciate. If you decide to rest a few lads for a game like that and lose, or get a bit of a beating, then a lot of the good work done already is gone. Your momentum is gone and the direction of the whole season might change. Anytime I'd hear people say – particularly about the round-robin format – that a team should rest more players, or that they'd be better off losing a particular game, it made no sense to me. Why do they think players are training like dogs for six months? It's to win games, and anything else is a betrayal of what's being preached in the group all the time.

That championship game was played at the intensity you'd expect. And of course Limerick wanted to win as well. They sprang Cian from the bench: the point I made about momentum applied to them too. So the win was something we appreciated. It showed we were on the right track, with four wins from four, the form was good and we felt we could get even better.

For all that, there were a couple of issues. Bonner Maher was injured that day, and he and Cathal Barrett ended up missing the Munster final. Playing in Limerick wasn't as much of a factor for us as Limerick's loss in the round robin was for them – their support is always passionate in the Gaelic Grounds but that day, the Munster final, they were really driving the Limerick lads on. After doing so well in the round-robin games we were almost a no-show that day. All the good things we'd been doing in the Munster championship were missing, and Limerick showed how good they were – they ended up winning the game by 12 points, which is a good trimming any day of the week.

In the long term it probably helped us, in that it gave us the motivation for the rest of the season, but that wasn't a consideration that evening. Looking back, maybe peaking five times in such a short period was a bridge too far. In previous years, four games, five games might have been enough to win you the All-Ireland itself. That year five games didn't get you out of Munster. We played to a very high standard in four consecutive games, which was great, and maybe for the fifth there was a subconscious feeling that we'd qualified for the All-Ireland series, so we could relax. Maybe. But at the end of the day, our performance fell flat. We'd put a lot into the four previous games, not just the opener against Cork but also against Clare in Ennis. That was a big game for us, going down to a hostile atmosphere and handling it, so a lot of energy had been used up in those four games.

There was a sign of the future in that Munster final too, in that we were level going into the final quarter but Limerick pulled away. They're a very well-conditioned team, very fit, but I felt we were also well conditioned. We didn't click the way we had in previous games and when they got on top they pulled away from us. We didn't play to the standard we'd set, and when that happens and a team comes with a surge, it's hard to match them. We didn't have that energy on the pitch, that freedom, and were just hanging in there. (It's easy to say you didn't have the legs for your opponents when they get a run on you like that, but it's not as simple as it looks. We'd have heard the same in 2021 when Limerick came hard in the second half and people were saying Tipperary's older players didn't have the legs – but I remember feeling better in the second half that day than I did in the first.)

That Munster final defeat brought us back to earth. I was on Kyle Hayes and he went through for a goal in the second half, so I had that to contend with. Noel was having a cracking year but he was taken off, and when I saw him go I remember thinking it wasn't our day. He'd been flying in the games beforehand and he was flying in the games after that one, which told me everything about our performance on the day. We regrouped in the dressing room after the Munster final. Liam stressed that, disappointing though it was, we'd been there before and come back, and we were still alive in the championship. And then he said something that stuck with me, and with the rest of the group: 'Remember, lads, if we get back to Croke Park, we will flourish.'

Liam was good to hit the right note like that, and a lot of the lads he was talking to were experienced enough to pack away the game and the disappointment. You have to be able to do that as a player, and if you can't, you need to learn pretty fast. It was disappointing, no doubt about it. There was a lot of talk about just how good Limerick were at that time – there still is – but we'd have felt confident heading down to the Gaelic Grounds: we'd have been mad to have a crack off them. The fact that we didn't perform, that we didn't show what we were fully capable of, that was the disappointment. If you do that, if you give it everything and you still come up short then you hold your hand up – the better team won, fair enough. But when you don't perform there are regrets. Liam and Eamon and the rest of the backroom knew that and were able to strike the right tone: 'Lads, relax for the evening, we'll regroup and meet for training and we'll be re-energised in Croke Park.' Again, good management – stressing that we belonged in Croke Park, that we could make our dreams come true there. That's subtle, because it's not rubbishing what happens in the Munster championship, but it's the kind of message you want to give to a disappointed team. You really belong on the biggest stage, that's what suits you.

And we took that on. We beat Laois in the quarter-final and faced into Wexford in the semi-final.

So much happened in that game, you'd nearly write a whole book about it. Davy Fitzgerald was Wexford manager and he's always in the spotlight. For us, Davy's personality wasn't an issue in 2019 – earlier in his management career that might have been more of a factor maybe, but by the time of that All-Ireland semi-final the focus was on how he was going to set his team up and how we'd set up against him. They played a sweeper, so management picked me to sweep against them and then gave the rest of the backs their match-ups. That was where our energy went because they'd won the Leinster final, and as a result there was huge momentum around that Wexford team, and huge belief. You felt something was coming, we knew they were going to bring a huge following to Croke Park. We knew we had to be absolutely perfect for it.

Whatever people might think, they had perfected that style of play, sweeping and attacking from deep, and it made the opposition think. It made *us* think closely about what we were going to do to counteract it, certainly – who's following who, who'll be free, all of that. It's hard to play against a team like that because in Wexford's case all of the players know their roles, but to an opponent it looks like chaos, and chaos is hard to deal with. That's why we had our jobs sorted out beforehand: I'd be free, Ronan would pick up Conor McDonald, Brendan would track Dee O'Keeffe, and so on. That was simple enough and we knew our roles well enough to allow us to go out and hurl.

And chaos is the right word. Take the first half, when it was hugely attritional in the middle of the field, with bodies crashing into each other. More than once I found myself meeting Wexford defenders coming up the field with the ball, 100 metres from where they should have been. At one stage Liam Ryan came the length of the field from full-back to hit a point, though in fairness Ronan did the same for us from the same position, going upfield and picking off a point at the other end. It was a great game to be part of, because so much of it was blood and thunder, fighting for every ball and seeing great scores. You didn't know where the game was going because you had your hands full just to get to grips with your own man or the next ball. But I had a belief in our forwards all the time – I felt if we were in with a shout in the closing stages they were good enough to get us over the line.

We were five down in the second half and John McGrath was sent off. We didn't dwell on that in the moment but I felt lads were driven on by it. Wexford took over for a few minutes as we adapted to being a man down; they got a goal and a couple of points. But we settled. I stopped being a sweeper and just picked up a Wexford forward, and we were still confident. Every time we won a free or there was a break in play we communicated with each other and reinforced the message: we are still in touch, we will get our chance, so keep going. I don't know if that belief came from having a good record against Wexford in big games, but it was a strength of ours that day, the feeling that if we hung in there, we'd get a chance.

And we did, picking them off point by point. We got good energy from the bench, with the subs making a difference when they came in, and even though the forwards should have been under pressure for space, being a man down, they were able to find room to shoot and kept reeling Wexford in. As the gap dropped from five to four to three points our confidence was growing and growing, but then Conor McDonald got another goal. That was a blow, and there were plenty of them in that game for us. There were the goals we had disallowed, the point that Brian Hogan saved going over the bar but was given when play was called back, John's red card ... there was a lot going against us, but the belief was very strong in the group. We weren't going to be beaten and we weren't going to lie down.

Where that came from specifically I don't know, but we were right. We hung in there: 3–20 to 1–28 at the finish. Gary Keegan was involved with us that year as a performance coach, and he was very beneficial in terms of our mindset and dealing with different scenarios. He's been involved with top professional teams over the years and he brought us to another level mentally, which showed in spades that day against Wexford.

At the final whistle we were jumping around the place like children, but that was out of pure relief at getting over the line, given the circumstances. That coexists with the experience – we'd been through enough to know that if we could stay in touch with Wexford we'd get the chances to win the game, but it also meant we appreciated the victory more than if we were only 19 or 20 years old, maybe. The value of a win like that can't be overstated. Definitely within the group the feeling would have been strong as we left Croke Park that evening that we'd win the All-Ireland. Knowing how deep we'd had to go to win was a massive boost to the group, and Liam appreciated that. Afterwards he spoke about keeping the head down as we still had a job to do, but he knew we were well aware of that. Particularly when it was Kilkenny facing us in the final.

I'd watched them beat Limerick in the previous day's semi-final. It was a godsend it was on that Saturday, because experienced as I was, putting down the day before a big match remained a trial. Myself and Ronan were still living at home and would be trying to kill the day without wasting energy, so having a match was a real treat. It was a great game, and even watching it I appreciated the quality on show, and having seen Kilkenny win it helped us to focus immediately after beating Wexford.

It's funny how the wheel turns. Myself, Brendan, Noel and Séamus were probably in the position that year that the likes of Henry Shefflin and Eoin Larkin were in back in

2009 and 2010 when we were starting. We were now the players with experience, and 2016 was a big part of that, the fact that we'd beaten them in that All-Ireland. That's confidence, not overconfidence. We knew well that they'd bring a huge challenge, as any Brian Cody team does, but the momentum was with us and the spirit was good.

We had a couple of meetings in the run-up to the final with the player group, but we weren't holding the younger lads' hands. The likes of Jake Morris and others had been in minor and under-20 All-Ireland finals and were well used to the big occasion. The semi-final against Wexford was good preparation with the crowd and atmosphere in particular, and that really showed in the younger players' readiness for the final. We'd have advised some of the younger lads about managing the build-up to the game, but a lot of the core group had been there since at least 2016 anyway. We were used to the rhythm of that week or two before the final, with the open night and the fitting for suits and all of that, so it didn't have an adverse effect on us. If anything it made us more excited about the game, and keener to get one over on Kilkenny. They'd got a good few over us, after all, and that was a big motivation.

The game itself was cagey enough to begin with, and was still fairly even up to the moment Richie Hogan was sent off for Kilkenny. I started at number seven but I got moved over onto Walter Walsh on the other wing halfway through the first half, so I was close enough to the incident. When it happened – Richie coming across Cathal Barrett out on the right wing – I felt immediately he was in trouble given the way his elbow went up, and he got a straight red. It was a massive turning point in the game, no doubt about it. We got a big lift, having an extra man, though we didn't designate someone specifically to play as the spare man because we couldn't guess which of us would have that opportunity.

In the end the full-back line organised the free man. Ronan picked up a Kilkenny forward, I marked Walter, and Brendan played T.J., which left one of our full-backs free at all times. As it happened, Kilkenny kept playing a very direct game. They'd started off with it and kept it going despite being a forward short, so we ended up winning a lot of those deliveries, fielding the ball cleanly or breaking it to the spare man. 'Bubbles' and Séamie got goals early in the second half, which meant Kilkenny had to get goals to have any chance, and that was a tall order when they were short a forward.

From the outside you might assume the lads were thinking, *This is over, we can take it handy*, but on the field we put the foot to the floor even more, if anything. It was coming from the sideline, from Liam and management, not to let up and to keep driving on. Every ball was fought for as though there was nothing in the game. We'd put so much effort into it that there was no way we were going to slip up. And it was Kilkenny we were playing – they'd dished out so much punishment to us over the years, we were going to keep going.

We won by 14 points in the end, conceding only 20 over the course of the game. There was great pride in that, in keeping them to only nine points in the second half because it was testament to the efforts of the backs. We won a lot of high ball in defence that day, which was a statement in and of itself: Kilkenny are renowned for their ability in the air but we dominated that aspect of the game, which showed how determined the lads were to keep the pressure on until the final seconds. The last minute or two were enjoyable, but we weren't counting down the time. The competitive element that gets you to an All-Ireland final in the first place doesn't fade in the game itself, and you keep your focus until the very end, the way you've been taught. Right up to the finish our thinking was, *I'm not going to be the one whose man get a point or a goal, I'm not letting the side down.* At the very end I got a cut and had to go off to get it seen to. We had the match won but I was bursting to get back on, I was roaring at the doctor to stitch me up so I could be on the field when the final whistle went. I didn't want to be off the pitch when the game finished – not so much because it's more enjoyable to be out there when the whistle goes, but because I wanted to keep contributing to the very, very end. That was the mindset we had, the one that had got us through the year.

All of the All-Irelands I won are different. For me, 2016 was the perfect victory, because we'd won the Munster final, played brilliantly all year and everything had gone smoothly. And it was a first for myself and Ronan to win together. There was a different texture to 2019. We'd been written off earlier in the year and had had to listen to a lot of talk about the need to bring in younger players. Coming back to win it with the older cohort made it all the more satisfying.

The Sarsfields

People who aren't affiliated to GAA clubs don't have a handle on what the club means to its members. And what the members mean to the club.

I can go back to the 2016 Tipperary county final and give a good example of what Thurles Sarsfields means. That year we beat Kiladangan in Semple Stadium. Now, you'd be high enough after winning the county anyway, but that was our third in a row. I was captain the same day, and we were inside in the social centre afterwards, like we always do – we go in there after a big game and have our meal together and a few drinks.

But the chairman of the club, Michael Maher – my father's cousin – and my uncle Paddy McCormack, who was coaching the team, came up to me that evening and said, 'Come on, they're looking for the cup up at the funeral.' We'd lost the great Mickey 'The Rattler' Byrne that weekend; I think he passed away a day or two before the game. The house part of the funeral was on the Sunday evening, the night of the match. I said, 'Grand, we'll only be half an hour or whatever,' so we went up along the Moyne Road at the top of the town, where Mickey lived. The family met us coming in with the cup and they were all delighted, and said that Mickey would have loved it. They're all mad Sarsfields people. And they brought us into the room where he was laid out, and they were putting the cup down in the coffin with him, because he was such a passionate Sarsfields man. I remember someone said, 'Will we take a picture?' and we were just all looking at each other for a second. But then we said, 'No, no.' There's a line that you can't cross, obviously.

It just goes to show, Mickey was such a staunch clubman that the family wanted the cup up to the house even though it was the day of his funeral. It was one of the stranger situations I found myself in after winning a trophy, though. People who are reared in GAA clubs can see that and they can appreciate it. Every club has people who are that passionate, and Mickey was one of them. He was also a great, great player with Tipperary in the 1950s, though to me as a child he was just one of the lads around the club. One of the loud lads around the club, admittedly. Mickey was always loud. He would make himself known and you knew he was around. He had that big, strong, outgoing personality, and any time he'd meet you he would say, 'You're a great man, and you remind me of the men who were full-back or half-back for Tipperary back in the '60s or '70s.'

That sticks in my mind because he was such a larger-than-life character to us. By the time I got up to 11 or 12, I was only starting to get an appreciation for who he was, and how famous he was in the GAA world. Myself and Mickey Cahill and a few others came on the team then and kept that run going, and the response was huge. Since then the likes of Mickey Byrne and Jimmy Doyle have passed away so that link is gone, but it's made stronger again because other people come in and keep it going. It's certainly not lost on me that we come from the club which gave the GAA Tony Wall, Jimmy Doyle, Tommy Doyle (the Rubber Man), Seán McLoughlin – the list goes on. Some of the greatest names in the GAA, and all from our club.

Thurles Sarsfields is one of the most famous clubs in

the GAA but as a child you don't appreciate it, obviously enough. It's just the club. But when I was coming up on 15 or 16 and beginning to progress from Dúrlas Óg to Sarsfields itself, it hit home. There's a wall outside the clubhouse up by Semple Stadium and it has portraits of all the Thurles Sars men who have been Tipperary captains – and there's a lot of them. How many other clubs would have that kind of a wall outside their club, with that much representation, with that many captains of All-Ireland-winning teams? I could have gotten my face up there but it wasn't to be. Hopefully Ronan will make it.

Those families are still in Thurles. Still famous. The Doyles, Jimmy and Tommy, Mickey Byrne, Tony Wall, Michael Murphy – and so many more. And because you'll still meet their family members around the town it just hammers that lesson home, you end up thinking, *Jesus, it's massive, so much representation in Tipperary over the years.* People never lose sight of that link between the Sarsfields and Tipperary either. It would always have been said to me, when we became more competitive and started winning All-Irelands between 2009 and 2019 with Tipperary, that when the Sarsfields are going well, Tipperary go well – and said by people outside of Thurles. Something like that would make anyone take extra pride in their club.

I judge how the club is regarded by the effort every team puts in to beat us. It's as if, every match we play, the whole place is mad to put one over on us. That is the greatest respect anyone can pay you. And if someone does defeat Thurles it's regarded as a massive victory for them. We always took that as a compliment. That was something that struck me when I came onto the club senior team. I'd seen it when we won the county in 2005 after 31 years; I wasn't involved that day, but I could see what it meant to people.

We're a bit like Tipperary in that we have a lot of local rivals bumping up against us. In the same way that Tipperary has a border with rivals such as Limerick, Cork, Waterford and Kilkenny, with Thurles being situated where it is we have other teams right next door no matter where we look. The likes of Drom and Inch, Loughmore-Castleiney, Holycross-Ballycahill and Moycarkey-Borris are all very close to us: any games with them are huge for them and huge for us. Upperchurch-Drombane is a big game for us any time we play them, and Clonoulty-Rossmore is another.

We haven't played Borris-Ileigh much over the years but Toomevara was a major obstacle for us for a long time, when they had the upper hand over us. Nenagh were keen rivals for a few years too, which isn't surprising given that the two of us are the big-town teams in the county. Everywhere you look there's a rivalry. A few of those teams have caught us over the years in games, and you see then what it means to them to beat us. In a funny way that challenge always made us stronger, though – we always knew we had to be going out at the top of our game, every day, because no matter what stage of the championship you were at, you always knew you were getting absolutely the best version of every other team.

Whether those rivalries ever go over the top ... maybe the playing group in Sarsfields before us had some hot and heavy days out, but when we came in as a group I don't think we had any poisonous rivalries with any teams. There certainly wouldn't have been any terrible sledging going on – if a lad lost his temper and told you to f— off in the heat of battle, that's fair enough, but there was never anything like the psychological warfare you'd hear about in inter-county football, the horror stories about fellas trying to get into their opponents' heads. Unless you count the fish and chips taunt. Over the years we'd have heard that a lot with the Sarsfields, other players or supporters with the, 'Sure ye're townies, the fish and chips.' I'm not sure why that was insulting, that you might have some fish and chips the odd time, but a few lads somehow felt it was a terrible blow to our confidence.

Some other clubs would sometimes suggest that we'd have an unfair advantage based on the size of Thurles – that we'd have a bigger pick than smaller clubs like Loughmore-Castleiney, which would be based around two small villages. It's true that there's a good population in Thurles by Irish standards, but the way we'd see it in the club, we have to work twice as hard to keep the numbers involved. In Thurles you have rugby, soccer, you have a second GAA club in the town – in smaller places around Tipperary those distractions don't exist. People outside the town might think there's more employment in Thurles to keep people in the town than other places, but we lose as many people to Dublin or Cork or Limerick as any other club, whether through education or work. A lot of those people don't come back: if you go through the teams I played in over the years you'd only pick two or three from each minor team that came through to keep playing at adult level.

Having said all that, I'd always have admired a club like Loughmore-Castleiney, who have the same group of players who play both hurling and football – and they always keep the hurling and football going together at a high standard. They caught us in 2021 in the county final, in the replay. That was the first time, I think, they beat us in a knock-out game and it was eventually going to come at some stage.

In fairness to them they have a fantastic spirit and ethos in the club, and I'd be friendly with the McGraths, Noel and John and Brian, and John Maher and a few more. (And of course that's where I lived in my early years.) You have to give them their dues. There is tremendous respect between the two clubs, obviously both teams would be mad to get one over the other but at the end of the day you'd still meet them for a pint after the match. That's not something you would do with every team you play.

One of the big challenges for us as a club was winning the county, obviously, but success there brings another challenge again – the Munster club. We were always keen to press on rather than regarding that competition as a bonus. We enjoyed the day or two after county finals; the Thurles Sarsfields Centre, Mackey's bar, Larry Fogarty's, the Tower Lounge and Lar Corbett's were our usual haunts, but you'd be straight back into training on the Tuesday or Wednesday, eager to take the next step.

I distinctly remember in 2012, when we won the county final – our third in four years – we celebrated as well as ever. We had two weeks to the Munster quarter-final against Kilmallock so myself and Mickey Cahill went to a few haunts to celebrate, but when we came back in on the Wednesday night Gary Mernagh, our coach, decided to run the celebrations out of us. Myself and Cahill led from start to finish on runs that felt like they'd never end. We'd had our fun but we weren't going to be stopped this time in Munster either.

We took a lot of criticism over the years for not doing more in Munster, not having more success, but we were never too far away. Any time we were beaten in Munster it was either in extra time or by a point. We won it in 2012, we lost the final in 2010 and the other years there were often only small margins in it. It was disappointing we didn't have another one or two Munster titles – but we always gave it a good rattle. It wasn't through lack of focus. Obviously you don't look past the county final when you're preparing for it, but the attitude was always right for Munster: 'Right lads, we can enjoy tonight but Tuesday night it's back to the field.'

Funnily enough, the best games I played for Sars were in Munster, and I often wondered why that was the case. Was it because other teams weren't as familiar with how I played? In a club match in your own county your team is dissected more, there is more analysis put into your performance and you're more familiar to the opposition anyway (and the same familiarity applies in reverse with your opponents, obviously). Whereas when you go outside the county that's not the case. You play a team from Cork or Limerick or

Waterford, that familiarity just isn't there. The two teams don't know each other and even though there's more video footage around nowadays than ever before, that's not nearly the same as playing a team for years, as happens in your own county. Because of that I always enjoyed playing the Munster club matches and I always got this freedom out of it: I felt my game went to another level in the Munster games.

Take 2010 as an example. We went down and beat Kilmallock at their place in a Munster club semi-final. That was a huge win. An unbelievable day. The ground was absolutely wedged, a heaving crowd, and it's a real hostile atmosphere when it's like that. People who know it will be familiar with the tight pitch with the wire all around, and on a big match day it feels like people are coming in over the wire on top of you. To go into that environment and dig out a win by a couple of points against a very good team was a milestone for us. I don't think any other team in Tipperary would have gone down there and won that game.

2010 was a fair campaign. As I say, I don't think any other team in Tipperary would have been able to do what we did that year. They'd have had to thaw out after that De La Salle game, for one thing – it was one of the coldest days I ever experienced. I remember going to Cork that day, the

Munster final, and being dubious all the way down that the game would even be played. It had been freezing cold weather all week and when we pulled up to the Rochestown Park Hotel it was no warmer than it had been in Thurles. We were saying among ourselves, 'No way is this going ahead – not a chance.' We'd got word in the cars on the way down that there was a possibility the match would be called off, and I remember supporters turning around and going back home because it was so bad.

When we got to Páirc Uí Chaoimh, though, the game was on, but when we walked out to see the pitch, the part underneath the old covered stand, which used to be in shadow, was completely frozen. I will never forget that game, playing on a field that was frozen solid in places. You couldn't even run on it in the boots. As the afternoon wore on, the sun was actually shining and, weak as it was, it started to defrost other parts of the field a little, but the whole of that side under the covered stand remained frozen. If you could keep the ball away from there you did so, because it was anyone's guess what would happen when it started bouncing around on the frozen ground.

De La Salle beat us – they would have had the likes of Kevin Moran, John Mullane, Bryan Phelan – but the scoreline tells you everything: 0–9 to 0–8 and we drove 17 wides the same day. We pucked the game away and were beaten by a point late on that Jake Dillon got. At least we came back in 2012 and won it below in Cork against the same opposition. That's another aspect of provincial club competition people miss out on – the more often you're there, the more experience you're getting. The team learns how to deal with different scenarios outside their own county, you're more familiar with your opponents if they're a team you've met before, as happened with us and De La Salle.

And we were really coming as a team at that stage. I was 23 and was getting more mature and more experienced, and you had older lads like Larry and Johnny Enright. Johnny was playing his last year but he was an absolutely unbelievable machine that season, while 'Redser' O'Grady was coming on for us as well. In 2012, a lot of things came together for the team. The age profile was just right, the preparations were good and we nearly had the perfect year. We won the Mid Division final when we beat Loughmore above in Templemore. Then we went on to the county quarter-final, and won that. Then after success in the semi-final we beat Drom and Inch in the county final, which was a big one for us. It was my first year as captain as well, which made it extra special.

Two weeks later, we went to Kilmallock and beat them, and then we defeated Cork Sarsfields who were flying – they had Cian McCarthy, Daniel Kearney, Eoin Quigley, Kieran Murphy, Conor O'Sullivan, Éanna Martin, Michael Cussen … they had a serious team. We'd won everything going. Including some off-field victories. In the final we were four up with time running out when 'Redser' O'Grady won a ball by the covered stand side – he went for a point and when it went over the bar he put his fist in the air to celebrate. We slagged him afterwards about the premature celebration but he told us he'd backed Sarsfields to win by five and he was celebrating the bet coming in. Some character.

There was a break then from the Munster club final, played in the first week in December, to the All-Ireland semi-final, which was played on my 24th birthday, 9 February. Managing that break is always a challenge for teams unless they've been in All-Ireland club semi-finals regularly. If anything we trained too well during the break and we came out flat in the match itself – Kilcormac-Killoughey from Offaly beat us by six points.

We repeated the feat in 2012, and having beaten Kilmallock we went on to play Cork Sarsfields in Thurles in the Munster semi-final, and that was another unbelievable game. Larry came through for us on that occasion with an incredible goal: he caught the ball in the middle of the field, ran the whole way through and buried it. That was the turning point. I was delighted for Larry that day, getting that goal – he'd been given plenty of stick over the years for not putting it in for the club, which was the greatest load of rubbish I ever heard – he's done things for the Sarsfields in that time that only his team-mates would appreciate. We won that game and then went down to Cork and beat De La Salle from Waterford in the final.

Different years, different challenges. The club can sometimes get sideswiped by outside influences. Take 2014. We won the county title in Tipperary that year as well, but it was a different scenario entirely because with Tipp we'd got to the All-Ireland final, but that went to a replay. Not only did that defer club action in the county, delaying the entire championship, it did so by three weeks. People forget there were three weeks between the All-Ireland final and replay, which created pressure in Tipperary to get the club matches completed.

When we came back to the club, the very next week we were playing with Sarsfields and we played the following eight weekends in a row. We were winning all the time, which was great, but after seven or eight weeks it was starting to take its toll. We won the county final easy enough against Loughmore-Castleiney, but there was no break: we had to go out again the next weekend and play Cratloe in Ennis. That wouldn't be easy even if you hadn't been out nine weeks in a row, All-Ireland final replay included. They had the Collinses, Podge and Seán, Conor Ryan and Conor McGrath, but the start of the game didn't help our cause. In the opening exchanges – literally the first few seconds – Denis Maher was sent off for us. The way I remember it, he got the ball and went to push a lad off but the referee said he made contact with the face. Gone. It was an absolute disgrace of a decision, one which still annoys me. We played the entire match with 14 players and we struggled. Between the fact that it was our tenth week on the trot and being down to 14 men straight away, we just didn't have it in us to get over the line.

At least that was disappointment based on a decision in a game. It stings, but you can put it in context. We had a very different situation in 2015. We got to the county final again and won a great game against Nenagh by a point – the experience of the big occasion was really an advantage. The draw for the Munster club meant we were taking on Na Piarsaigh in the Gaelic Grounds two weeks later. Limerick champions, full of inter-county players, playing in their back yard? Our attitude would have been bullish: bring it on.

We were back training and buzzing for Na Piarsaigh the Saturday after the county final – and we were working on a few tactical things. At one stage we were running through a backs and forwards drill and Jack Griffin fell in for a minute or two. Jack was an army officer and our fitness coach – a really fit man, a good hurler in his time and Sars to the core – and during the drill he came in at me as a dummy runner, the way forwards try to drag you out of position on their own puckouts. He was mirroring the movement to pull me out of position and we were having a bit of craic with him, pulling and dragging – the kind of stuff that happens in training every week of the year.

It was Halloween the same day, so we all had a good laugh in the clubhouse before breaking up and going our separate ways. The Rugby World Cup final was on and Australia were taking on New Zealand, so myself, Ronan and my cousin Denis were out in our house watching it; we were going to go into the swimming pool after for a recovery session. Then the phones started buzzing. Messages. Jack Griffin involved in a road traffic accident. We were hoping he was alright but details were scarce: had he just had a tip in the car?

We were in the pool when information started filtering through. Jack was out for a run. A car hit him. He was in hospital. Then Denis looked up from his phone: 'Jesus, Jack is after dying.'

Word got around then. It had happened at the top of the road by the golf course. He was going for a run and was just turning for home when he was struck by a car. That shocked us all. In the morning he'd been messing with us in training as we practised puckouts, and in the afternoon he was killed 500 metres from his own front door, leaving a young family behind.

It turned the whole town upside down, never mind the club. We were distraught but Jack's family were shattered, obviously. Jack was a young, fit man and well known in Thurles, and the fact that he was in the army meant there was a huge army involvement and presence in the town for the funeral as well. The Griffin family are staunch members of the Sarsfields, and Jack had married into the Malonys, who own Thurles Racecourse and are mad Sars people too, so that all made the crowd on the day even bigger. Thurles came to a complete standstill, which was a fitting tribute to Jack.

In terms of the game against Na Piarsaigh, that wasn't on anyone's radar. Our manager, Tommy Maher, was best friends with Jack so he was heartbroken. No one was in the right frame of mind to think about playing a match. In fairness to Na Piarsaigh, they immediately agreed to postpone the game for a week. It's no more than you'd expect from any club in that situation but it was still good to have that gesture, it showed that in the GAA people can keep things in their proper context. When we went back training we told ourselves we had the motivation of Jack's memory, but deep down the lads were drained. You were going from being so high after winning the county final and the mood being so good, to dealing with the grief from your friend's passing. Basically, the whole thing just went from under us. While we were in contention for a lot of the game, when it came down to the crunch we just couldn't raise it; we didn't have it in us, mentally. Lads were simply all over the place from the preceding couple of weeks. Afterwards the dressing room was eerily quiet. No one spoke, really, because it was clear that everyone was thinking the same thing: *Let's just get this over with and get out of here.*

That fed into the following season, 2016, and Tommy Maher was a huge part of that. Seamus Quinn was great for us over the years with Sars as manager, and we won a Munster club championship under him. Michael 'Glossy'

Gleeson was also a vital part of our club. I had Glossy as coach and manager throughout my whole career since under 14, winning county finals across all the grades, a great man also. But Tommy was one of the best managers I've played under, if not the best: Sars to the core. He had my uncle Paddy in as coach and my uncle Connie, from the other side of the family, as a selector, and they really hit the right notes all year: three massive clubmen. Tommy laid it on the line early in the year on behalf of the club, the team, the supporters. He said we wanted to win the county final and added that we had this other motivation: Jack. There were pictures of Jack on the dressing-room wall and notes of things he would have said to us. We used that as motivation and that year I felt we weren't going to be beaten.

That's something you often hear from players after winning a title, but it was never truer than that year. We did go on to win the county final but people don't realise that Jack gave the speech that put us in the right frame of mind for the game. In the 2015 county final, the week before he was killed, Jack gave the final few words before we went out. That's when teams get revved up for the game – the plans and tactics have all been absorbed, and it's time to put the players in the frame of mind for combat. And that's what Jack did that day, he put it on the line for lads in the dressing room in Semple Stadium: then out, down the tunnel, and onto the field.

What we didn't realise at the time, though, was that Mick Clohessy, our masseur, who has been our masseur for as long as I've been playing with the club, recorded Jack's speech on his phone. We've often asked him since what possessed him to do it, and he'd say, 'I don't actually know, it just came into my head.' So while Jack was delivering this unbelievable speech about what the club means to people and the need to win, Mick was recording. And a week later Jack was killed. Fast forward 12 months and we were counting down to the 2016 final. Obviously we'd had this motivation all year, to win the county for Jack and his family, and the team was going well, but that Saturday, the day before the final, we met up for a few pucks.

Nothing unusual in that. Teams often get together to iron out a few things and give lads a last chance to get their eye in. But Tommy brought us into the dressing room when we were done pucking around. Fair enough, we thought, some general instructions for the game the following day. When everyone sat down he took out a recorder and hit 'play' and the whole backroom team, all the panel, the management team, were all there sitting down in a big group in the Sars dressing room listening to Jack's speech from the year before. You could see that lads were getting emotional, unsurprisingly. It was powerful. Tommy didn't go over the top with it, though. He left it play out, two or three minutes, and when it stopped no one said a word. Then Tommy got up and looked at us all, and everyone stood up. Nothing was said, because nothing needed to be said. There was a sense of, *Right, this is it.*

We all just went home and came back the following day to the stadium and beat Kiladangan, 0–27 to 1–15. The previous year everything had happened so quickly we didn't have the strength in us as a team to win the Na Piarsaigh match, but in 2016 we had it right. Tommy and the boys worked it well when it came to motivation and didn't overdo it. They didn't play that recording for us on the day of the game because they knew we'd have been all over the shop. They judged it correctly, and it was important to get that right. Not so much to win a game, but to do justice to the memory of our friend. And lads bought into that. They knew that even if they weren't performing well, hurling-wise, they weren't going to stop working hard for the team, that they'd give their all. It was important to produce a performance that Jack would have been proud of, because we were so proud of him.

I was honoured to be captain of that team. Over the

years when we won county finals, our biggest supporter, Declan Ryan, would always have lifted the cup with me, but on that day in 2016 we gave the honour of raising the Dan Breen Cup to Jack's three lovely girls – Laragh, Isabelle and Emma. They deserved that privilege at least.

The club means everything to me. I had great times with Tipperary, memories I wouldn't swap for anything, but Sarsfields is family.

One of my great friends, Thomas Callanan has been secretary of the club since 2005. Thomas is wheelchair bound. In 2002 he made his senior debut for the club at corner back on a Sunday afternoon and by the middle of that week, he was seriously injured on a bike on his way to work in Dublin.

Life changed that quick for him and he could no longer play, but he changed the club and its mentality. It's no coincidence the club has gone through one of its most successful periods with him in charge. He basically ran the club. We don't have far to look for inspiration. We just look at Thomas.

My first county final win in 2009 was huge. We beat Drom and Inch and it was fantastic, but because I knew what had gone on for years in the club through my family, and how much they wanted to win a county final, I really appreciated it. Sars had previously won in 2005 and then there was a bit of a drought before we won again in 2009 and set off on our own journey.

In 2012 I was captain when we triumphed in the Munster club, a title we'd never won before, so that was unbelievable. But to win four in a row from 2014 to 2017 – that obviously produced a lot of special memories outside of going up to Mickey Byrne's coffin with the cup. If 2016 stands out, with what happened to Jack, that's understandable, but the club means more than just county finals and big days out. For instance, Jack wasn't the only person we were playing for in 2016. Andy Rossiter was our kit man for years, a pure character and a great hurler in his day. If you met him on the street you'd have said to yourself, *A pure grumpy lad*, but he was a great personality in the club. He suffered illness and passed away in 2015 – another major part of the club gone suddenly (his sons are playing now and they're serious players). He died the same year as Jack, so we felt as a club we were getting hit the whole time. And as a family we had our own bereavement to deal with that year.

My first cousin Caroline was unwell for a while with breast cancer before passing away in 2015, so she was a motivation for us – me, Ronan, our cousin Denis and our uncle Connie, who was a selector. Caroline was always behind us, whether we were playing for Sarsfields or for Tipp, playing in Croke Park or in Semple Stadium, so within the family we had that particular drive to do well in her memory.

When you see your family go through something like that with Caroline, it hits you hard. Her mam Judy, our aunt, is an unbelievably strong woman. They were always great supporters of ours so to give them some small bit of happiness by winning those games was very important to us. When you see a team win a county final you aren't usually aware of those kinds of motivating factors. Between Jack, Andy and, in our case, Caroline, we weren't short of a cause that year or other years. Being part of a club means drawing all that together for the common good. If you're a member of a club, though, you already know that.

Blindsided:
how a career ends

We played Kiladangan in the county semi-final in October 2021, and won by two points.

I was happy with my performance that day, it was one of my best seasons, and everything was going great. Kiladangan had won the county title the previous year, we'd been down for a couple of seasons, so it was great to get back on track.

Particularly the way the whole world had shut down in March 2020 due to covid.

I'd had a great start to training that year and was feeling determined to back up our good year in 2019, and hungry for more success.

When covid hit and we had to deal with travel restrictions and social distancing, it wasn't ideal to be living out in the country. Because I was determined not to let my fitness and sharpness slip, myself, Ronan, Uncle Paddy – who lived next door and was no stranger to coaching – and my cousin Michael undertook some savage hurling sessions out the back of the house whenever restrictions were lifted enough to allow us to do it.

All Paddy needed was decent-sized space – which we had – cones, balls, a wall, and a few bodies.

We trained ourselves to death during those periods. At times we had to crawl back in from the garden afterwards. Overdoing it? Probably, but also doing everything possible to help us be ready for whenever we were allowed to live again. And we carried the benefit of those savage sessions whenever we could from 2020 into 2021 and back to a county final, which was a great way to wind up the year.

That Kiladangan game was a Saturday evening, and we had two weeks to the final against Loughmore-Castleiney. The week after the semi-final we trained away, and Mark Dowling and Liam Egan, our trainers – two Kilkenny men – wouldn't be taking it easy on us in the run-in to the county final. A couple of days' recovery then a few tough sessions to sharpen us up. The Sunday before the final we met up and had a good, tough training session for an hour or so. Part of the session was conditioned games, where you're getting belted and hit hard time and time again, but nothing sticks out. I don't remember being on the receiving end of a particularly tough challenge or shoulder, maybe because there were so many of them.

But when I woke up that Monday I felt off, and as the day wore on I was getting worse – headaches, dizziness, all of that. Covid was rampant at the time, so that was my first concern. I was convinced I had it, but I didn't want to miss the county final for anything, and I was thinking I'd lie low for a few days. On Tuesday I rang management and said I didn't feel well, so Mark Dowling, the manager, said to stay away from training that evening. I stayed away for the rest of the week, as it turned out, because I wasn't feeling much better. There was a small improvement, maybe because I wasn't doing anything physical, but not by much. I was conscious that we'd asked my father to come home from Wales for the match, and I went down to Clonmel to collect him on the Saturday. I remember bringing him back to my house in town to watch Ireland play New Zealand in rugby, and I could barely focus on what was happening on the television. Everyone was sitting down watching the game and having the craic, and I was thinking, *This isn't the best preparation for a game*. The TV screen was blurred and fuzzy: not good.

The following day I headed up to the stadium for the game and I was all over the shop. In the warm-up when I was going for the ball I was missing it, stepping over it, missing passes – not ideal preparation when I was going out to mark John McGrath, who was having an unbelievable season for Loughmore-Castleiney. During the parade around the field I was looking about: everything was a blur. The game itself was a nightmare. In the first half at one stage I had John McGrath in on me one-on-one, and when the ball shot out to the corner I was trying to get a hold of him, just in order to find where he was. I was only managing to knock the ball away from him in order that someone else could gather it. I was beating my man to the ball – it was just that I couldn't see the ball when it was in front of me.

It was a depressing experience, because I felt if I was fully fit I could have contributed a lot more to drive the team on and made a real difference. The game ended in a draw, which made it worse; you'd always think you could have done some little bit more to turn things in your favour. I told the management after the game that I felt bad, so we

decided I'd have a Covid test. The panel was going back
to the clubhouse for a meal and a drink – it was a two-
week break to the replay – but I went home with Claire
and booked myself a Covid test for the Monday. On the
Tuesday afternoon the result came back – negative.

I went to the doctor and he suspected vertigo, so he gave
me medication for that. I had a week and a half to the
replay, so he told me to rest up ... but the competitive
urge kicked in, and I'd hop up on the Wattbike instead of
going to training. I ended up nearly killing myself for an
hour on the bike, but when I'd get off it I'd have to lean
on it to stop from falling over. So management insisted
that I rest, pure and simple, the week of the game. And
the symptoms started to clear up: I was thinking, *Yes, the
tablets are kicking in*.

In the warm-up for the replay, although I wasn't as dizzy
as I'd been before the drawn game, I still wasn't right.
Still not 100 per cent. And in the parade, the same thing:
blurred vision.

In the game itself, at times I could see a couple of different
balls dropping in together, my vision was so bad. I was
beating my man out to the ball regularly, but I wasn't able
to gather it. In previous games I'd knock the ball down,
gather it and be gone, but I couldn't get the ball into my

hand at all. As the game wore on I actually came into it more, trying my best to get us over the line, but at the very end I was out in the corner chasing John McGrath, with the game level. He won the ball and I challenged him, and if I'd been healthy I don't think I'd have given away the foul, but the whistle went. He slotted it over from a tight angle, and the game was over. Gone.

Colm Bonnar, the new Tipperary manager, rang me and asked me to see the new physio for an MOT. I had an ankle injury that was niggling at me, so I went in to see John Casey for a scan, and he suggested taking January off. That that would have me right and raring to go for the 2022 season. Grand. Paul Ryan rang me two weeks before I was due to go back, and asked me how I was.

'The finest,' I said. 'Can't wait to get back.'

'You know what we'll do,' he said. 'We'll get a neck and head scan done to make sure everything's right. Maybe there's an old concussion there that might be bothering you, so if we get all of that cleared up we can drive on then.'

No bother.

I had an MRI in Barringtons' in Limerick on my neck and head, and a couple of days after that I got called in by University Hospital Limerick for a CAT scan. I told them I'd had the scan in Barringtons' already, but they still wanted me in. Grand. Off with me. A few days later the ultrasound department from UHL got on to me for an ultrasound on my neck.

At that stage I was asking if it was me they wanted, given I'd had a scan there just a couple of days earlier.

'Yes, Pádraic Maher, 02/09/1989,' they confirmed. 'This is different – we want to look at the veins and arteries in your neck.'

I went along but I rang Paul Ryan about it, and he said he'd look into it. The hospital referred me to a specialist – Tony Moloney in Henry Street, Limerick. I was to go and see him.

In the meantime there was another development. Myself and Claire got engaged and we were due to head up to her home place in Ennis for an engagement party with her family and friends. And of course the appointment with Tony Moloney was for the same Friday. That was grand – in to see him at one o'clock and then up to Ennis for the party. Perfect.

I saw Tony on the Friday as arranged: nice man, very professional. He ran a few reflex tests and then pulled out the scans and put them on the screen. 'You're probably wondering why I sent you for all those scans,' he said.

'I thought you were mixing me up with someone else,' I told him.

'No, I just wanted to get a full picture so I could show you everything, so that it'd all make sense.'

He showed me a scan of my brain, and there were dots visible – dots he said shouldn't be there.

'That's why you were getting dizzy spells,' he said. 'They've drifted up from your neck. You've had an arterial dissection with one of the arteries in your neck and little blood bubbles have drifted up into your head. It's like having a ministroke, causing you to get dizzy.

'Every time you were hit, these bubbles were drifting up into your brain.'

Now, when you have a doctor telling you there are bubbles drifting into your brain giving you ministrokes, you start sitting up straight in the chair. He was talking about the artery and he showed me the scan, where I could see a flap of skin, for all the world that shouldn't be there.

Eventually I asked the question. 'Are you telling me to stop playing?'

He sat back and said, 'I'm not going to be the one to tell you to stop. But if you were my brother or my son I'd be telling you that's it. Stop.'

'But what are you telling me to do?' I said.

'I'm not the one to make that call,' he said. 'You were lucky, really, that there was only this much damage. It could have been much worse.'

I rephrased my question: 'Should I stop playing with the county and just go back to the club?'

'This could happen anywhere,' he said. 'With the club as easy as with the county.'

He told me he couldn't pinpoint what had happened, or when. It could have been at that final training session before the county final or it could have happened months before. It's associated with whiplash in a car crash, when your neck twists one way or the other from the impact. The way he explained it, if someone called you and you turned to answer them quickly, it could happen, but that'd be very rare. It's a rare condition anyway, but a collision is usually responsible. In my case I could go on playing and the next time I had a big collision it mightn't happen, or the time after that, or the time after that. Or it could happen in a Munster championship game in Semple Stadium: I could collide with someone and end up on the ground with a major stroke. He advised me to think about it and to talk to my family – to talk to whoever I wanted to – and he also gave me his number and said to give it to any doctor who wanted to contact him.

I walked out thinking, *Is that it?*

I rang my mother, because she knew I was going to meet the specialist. 'How did you get on?' she asked.

'I think I'm done, mother.'

She got upset, and I had to explain that the specialist had said I'd been having ministrokes, all of that.

I rang Claire after that and in fairness she said, 'Look, we'll cancel the evening.'

'We can't cancel,' I said. 'Sure if we do that people will be wondering what's going on. The whole thing is organised, the family and friends are all there.'

So we went ahead, and in a way it was a good idea. I met a lot of people I'd never met before, her family and friends, and had a couple of drinks, and it went out of my head to a certain extent for the evening. Claire kept asking me how I was, and we got through it, but the next morning after breakfast I had to head off early. Phone calls to make.

On the way home I rang Brendan Murphy. He'd been our team doctor with Tipperary for a few years and he hurled with Offaly himself; I'd have been close enough to him. At that stage he was well gone from the set-up but he'd always said, 'If you've an issue, give me a ring.' We had the craic for a few minutes and then he asked how I was. He knew I hadn't been 100 per cent in the county final a few weeks earlier, so I told him about the scans and the specialist and the second I mentioned 'arterial dissection' he said, 'Uh-oh.'

I told him what the specialist had said.

'You have to stop,' Brendan told me.

He's a hurler himself and he knew me and what playing and training meant to me, but he said it straight out. 'You're 32, turning 33, you've had a great career. What are you gaining from this? I know it's a nightmare not being able to get back to the club, and I know you want to talk to people, but ...'

He knew I'd respect his opinion, but I also wanted to check in with Paul Ryan. Paul had been in touch with Tony Moloney, so he knew the score. When I asked him he was straight out as well: 'You have to stop. I'm coming from the doctor's side of things, but I'm also coming at this from a personal perspective. You've given so much to the county, so much to the club, but you just have to give up.'

I asked if he was telling me to retire, and he said he was: 'I can't stand over you going out to play a championship game for the Sarsfields in a few months' time knowing you have this issue with your neck, knowing there's a possibility this could happen.'

I went home, out to the mother's house because she

was cooking the dinner – chicken, very nice – and my uncle Paddy came in. I'd be close to him and he'd have been involved in hurling with us for years, and when I told him he was straight up: 'Pádraic, don't be thinking about hurling or anything like that. This is all about your health. You have to listen to the doctors.' My mother was the same. She was devastated for me that my career was coming to an end but obviously she'd be thinking of my health. So I had three doctors telling me to stop – my two GPs, if you like, and a specialist in the area. And in the meantime, Tony Moloney got in touch with Dr Éanna Falvey, who's the chief medical officer with World Rugby. Éanna was out in New Zealand but he responded that, based on the information he was given, the best thing for me to do would be to finish. I imagine he'd have seen a lot of those types of injuries in rugby.

Now, despite all of that, nothing would do me but to ring all the doctors again that Monday morning. The National League was beginning the following weekend and I'd had a couple of days to think about the whole thing, so I wanted to get it out there and move on. Claire suggested a fourth opinion, or a fifth, to try to work through all the options before making any announcements. Eventually I rang Brendan Murphy again and asked for his opinion again. 'It's your decision,' he said. 'But I think you'd be 100 per cent wrong to go back. What are you getting from that apart from putting yourself at risk? Go running, or go to the gym, or play squash or golf or something. But don't go back.'

And because I trusted him 100 per cent I took that on. I rang Paul Ryan again; he'd been back in touch with Tony Moloney. Paul said it was straightforward – his view hadn't changed.

That evening myself and Claire sat down and typed up my retirement statement. The following morning, Tuesday, we sent it out, and that was it. A career over when you press 'send' on the computer.

Different strokes: how you can tell the county by the way they play

Something that often pops up when I'm chatting to people about hurling is the notion of different styles and different approaches to the game. There are a lot of similarities now in how counties play the game – you rarely, if ever, see a defender hit the ball as long and as high as they can, because there's such a premium on possession. No team wants to give the ball away and everyone is trying to mind it. Because of that there are a lot of common factors – lads giving short passes, angling the ball into the corners, holding onto it until something opens up – but for all of that there are differences too. Every county has its own traditions, its own heritage, and those come out in the way they play.

That's the key – teams have certain tactics they share but they have to put their own stamp on them. I think Clare like to get lads behind the ball, for instance, and Galway get lads behind the ball as well. Limerick even get lads back around the ball, but it's more like they have different options then. If Limerick win the ball back, they have a choice – they can do the running or they can launch a ball in, whatever one is on for them.

So even though Galway and Limerick can get players behind the ball like Clare, they can also be more physical. Limerick are the dominant team at the moment, All-Ireland champions multiple times, and the champions will always dictate the trends. With them it's not as straightforward as sit back, invite the opposition on and then turn them over and counter-attack. They just seem to have different ways of playing depending on the situation, because they're obviously coached very well by John Kiely and Paul Kinnerk. But they also have other advantages.

They have a noticeably high work rate, they go back down the field to support their backs, but they're also very good at getting back up the field, getting in on the ball in numbers. Their wing-forwards can pick up scores at the opposite end of the field because they're accurate, but also because they work so hard for each other. They crowd the middle area, they turn you over there, they get the bodies around, and then they like to look up and hit cross-field balls into the corners.

Immediately, then, if you're up against them you have a challenge. They make you think a lot about your options, because you either have to go with your player if he tracks out the field, or if you sit back, then they just play these little triangles in the middle of the field and pick off scores at their ease. The best way to play against them – for us or for any team, I think – is to crowd out the middle and try and win that battle zone. But that's easier said than done! For instance, if you're marking someone like Gearóid Hegarty, you have to stick or twist. He's going to head back down the field: do you go with him? If you don't, then he's back in that battle zone – getting on breaks or getting a hand pass off or receiving one, or he's turning bodies over himself in that area, he's so strong. Do you let him off? If you do, then you really need to have your forwards come out the field to where they can tackle him and let you sit back.

That's where the coaching comes in. When I say Limerick are very well coached that sounds like a cliché, but you can see it in how they operate – that's not an accident. To have the success they have in the middle third the whole team has to work in sync, and that's all down to preparation. In the case of Hegarty, for instance, there's no point in the forwards staying down in their positions, letting him drift back the field and following him down yourself, because then the ball goes directly in behind you, where you should be. There's space left when you move out the field, and Aaron Gillane's coming out onto that ball and scoring.

I'm not sure if that's something people realise – not about Limerick working together as a team, but that as the opposing side you have to do the same, and sometimes that breaks down. When it breaks down the whole thing is in disarray, because for the approach to work everyone has to do their job; if someone gets their job wrong, everyone else is left exposed. If someone doesn't know their role it can look ugly very fast. That definitely comes down to coaching, and probably one or two times we went up against them we weren't up to the level, tactically, that we should've been. Not always. In other games I thought we showed very good glimpses of getting on top of them. In 2020 we played them in a league match in Semple Stadium and we were all over them for most of that game, but we let them back into it and they won it. You can see that there are ways to get at them, but you have to be consistent for the full 70 minutes.

One of the big challenges is the physical element that Limerick bring. They're big players, they're physical, and it's about that middle area, between the two 45s, where a lot of the congestion and the physicality is; it's so punishing. You need to be able to stand up to them for the entire game. Are they the strongest team I've come up against? They are. Not that Kilkenny weren't physical when we were taking them on around 2009, 2010. They were, and they even played a game that wasn't dissimilar, when their half-forwards used to come back down the field. But there was one big difference in how that Kilkenny team approached the game – they were far more direct with their delivery. They knew their forwards were all well able to win the ball or were expecting the ball to come in quick, whereas Limerick tend to get players back and play a few little short passes. They're very good at those triangles: hand pass, hand pass, hand pass, then deliver the ball into the space that's left in the corner. They work it to a place from which they can deliver to their forward the best ball possible. You see the balls

Aaron Gillane gets in front of him in most games – they're nearly unplayable for a defender.

That's a big difference between the old Kilkenny side and Limerick, who play the higher percentage balls for the forward, whereas Kilkenny were getting lads back to win the ball and deliver it quick. To me there's more chance to do damage when you get the ball in quick, actually, the way Kilkenny played. But there are other differences too. I remember Brendan Cummins saying years ago that Kilkenny didn't really have a puckout plan because they were all big enough and strong enough to either win the ball or at least contest it. What's funny is that Limerick are as big as that Kilkenny side, or bigger, but the ball is more directed when Nickie Quaid takes a puckout. With Limerick there's always a lot of movement off the puckout, or they're moving into space. They're really mobile – very rarely is Nickie just banging a ball back out to someone. Whereas with Kilkenny traditionally that movement wouldn't be as sophisticated; it's almost as if the ball is going long and a Kilkenny lad is expected to fight for it.

That might sound like good news for defenders, but the opposite is the case. If Aaron Gillane or John McGrath or Conor Whelan gets the ball delivered out in front of them, one bounce and into their hand, then the back is in huge trouble. I know myself if I was in that position it's all over: they have the upper hand. The way hurling has gone now, with the middle third of the field a battle zone, it means there are a lot of bodies out there. In turn, there's space at either end of the pitch for both full-forward lines. So if the ball is somehow worked out to a player who can deliver the ball to the full-forward line, a 70/30 ball, there's a fair chance it can't be defended by a full-back, as simple as that. You see Aaron Gillane as the perfect example in a lot of games – the ball he gets is nearly undefendable, coming in on a bounce for him once he's made that first run. That's why it's so important that your players out the field are doing the business and stopping the delivery being too good.

I marked Séamus Flanagan in the Munster final in 2021 and thought I was doing a fine job. He got two points in the first half, but the two balls were just knocked out in front of him and he got out, he made the run, ball into hand, and he hit it over his shoulder. Now, you'd be saying to yourself in that situation, *I'm trying to do my job here – he's striking off the back foot over his shoulder*. He scored them, fair enough, but you're doing all you can do – it's just that the ball coming in is undefendable. When Limerick played Galway in the 2022 All-Ireland semi-final Gillane had three or four points racked up in no time in the first half. The ball coming in was immaculate. His man, Daithí Burke, had a fine game, but the points Gillane was getting came about because the ball was being worked to the man out the field and it was being pinpointed in.

That's the challenge for a defender against a top team. There's an acre of open ground in front of you, but you can't play from the back or you'll be destroyed. You have to be brave and take the step and go out to win the ball, but Limerick know that's your plan. It's fine to say to the inside-backs, 'You know it's coming, there's a cross-field ball on its way,' but that's the time Limerick know if you're making a step, you can be caught. Those forwards are cute enough to take a step the other way and the ball comes in the other direction. And as a back you're toast.

Other teams bring other challenges. Waterford didn't have a great 2022 but in the last couple of years they've been there or thereabouts. They caught us in 2021 with a very high-energy game. They were running the ball from deep, they're very athletic, so you need a lot of energy to play against them. But it's different to Limerick. Playing against Waterford feels unstructured – you have the sense that you could end up anywhere on the field. At times it's like even Waterford players don't even know what they're going to do or where they're going to end up. It's just a free-for-all, whereas Limerick know where they're moving to at all times. Their forwards, inside-forwards, they know what they're doing, the moves they're making, where they're supposed to be situated on the pitch. Their back line is very structured. Their two midfielders are sitting in front. They work to a way of playing. Obviously it doesn't always work out like that, but they have an idea of the template they're working from. Whereas you always feel like Waterford could end up anywhere. Jack Fagan could be going back into the back line, likewise he could be wing-forward, wing-back. Austin Gleeson? Don't even ask me where he plays. You could say with confidence that it'd be Conor Prunty for Waterford as full-back and Tadhg de Búrca for centre-back, and the rest of them could be anywhere. The fact that they're very unstructured has its own challenges. It's hard to play against because Waterford seem to play well under that system, where they're given the licence to do what they want. And of course there's your own confidence against a particular team as well. We'd have always felt confident going against Waterford – the 2021 game was the first time they'd beaten us in the championship in a while.

We'd be confident going up against Cork as well. In their own way they play a very structured game, but it's a short game with a lot of passing, so you need a lot of energy to play against them. To me, though, if you stopped Cork's short game, you felt like they were going to crumble. Now, they caught us once or twice. They beat us in 2017, we drew with them in 2018, beat them in 2019, we beat them in 2016 and in 2014 … so yeah, we had the upper hand really. And while we'd be confident playing them, you'd expend a lot of energy in those games because they're very fast, especially in the forwards, and their movement is good. They're always moving for puckouts and in general play.

I didn't play against Cork when they were as extreme as they are now at this short passing game. They used to play the short passing game when I was playing against them too, but probably one or two short passes and it was hit directly into the forward. They'd try and drag you out and then hit the ball in, whereas now it's very nearly a matter of passing the ball into the goal. The other big thing playing against Cork over the years was their puckout strategy. That's when they used to make specific plans for it and they'd be running everywhere and they're so fast – that was the most difficult thing about playing them. Usually, though, we said if we could break down Anthony Nash's puckout, we'd beat them, and more often than not, when we did break it down, we did beat them. But in 2017, they definitely ran us, and the key to that was their puckouts. I was playing half-back that day and they ran us all over the place and brought us everywhere, and it was just impossible to get to grips with them. In the second half we were fighting to get back in but weren't able to, whereas in 2016 we got on top of their plan and won. Even in 2018 we played them in Thurles and they were beating us well, but we brought it back because we dealt with the puckouts in the second half. We became more aggressive on their restarts and we actually got a draw with them when we probably shouldn't have. Again, it all came down to the puckouts. Crack those and you were nearly there.

Clare are different again. They have one player who is so central to all their plans. Tony Kelly is a brilliant hurler but when you come up against Clare it's an obvious point to focus on, formulating a plan to limit him as much as possible because the team revolves around him so much. To illustrate that, we played them in 2019 and it was a case of designating someone to mark him – Brendan Maher in this case – and for the rest of us to just do our job. We felt if we took Tony Kelly out of the game we'd go a long way to beating Clare. And to this day I feel the same. The 2022 All-Ireland semi-final against Kilkenny is another good example of that. Clare have other good forwards as well, of course they have. I'm not disrespecting them. But Tony Kelly is out of this world at times, so you take him out of the game and Clare suffer. The stats show he's contributing 12, 13, 14, 15 scores in every game, so naturally enough, you take him out of it and their scoring drops.

It's unusual nowadays because most inter-county teams have a spread of scorers. It's usually the free-taker who ends up with nine or ten points, but you're looking for everyone to chip in as well to get over the line.

Here's the compliment. When it comes to individuals, of all the teams we played against, we wouldn't have pinpointed any other player as much as we did Tony Kelly. But we didn't play Clare as much as you might think. We played them in 2011 but then not until the All-Ireland quarter-final in 2017. Then they beat us in 2018, and the following year we beat them.

Face to face: marking the best

Other teams too had players you'd be aware of, such as Joe Canning with Galway, T.J. Reid with Kilkenny. At times we'd pay attention to Cian Lynch with Limerick, but usually with those players it was a case of: 'If he's in a certain line, someone takes him,' or 'If he's in this area, someone in particular takes him.' But the player we put the most emphasis on was Kelly, and absolutely it's a compliment to him.

Galway were structurally and physically not dissimilar to Limerick but played a slightly different game, one that was probably dictated by the players they had available to them. They were always going to be a bit more direct because they had big men up front. The likes of Johnny Glynn and Joe Canning were both big men. Conor Cooney and Joe Cooney were big, Cyril Donnellan was playing for Galway when I started and was another big man at centre-forward. So they were obviously going to put the ball in high over your head rather than playing sharp, short balls around the middle of the field. Why wouldn't you? They were physical athletes, so when playing Galway, you have to be that bit more physical and confrontational – to change your game a little to suit what they brought.

Another questions lads always ask is one of the most obvious: Who's the best I came up against? Tony Kelly is up there in the top three, definitely. Even though I believe we had him fairly well shackled when Tipp played them, you just have to look at what he's able to do on a hurling field, it's absolutely ridiculous at times. He has the touch but he has speed as well, a turn of pace that lads like Joe Canning, Patrick Horgan or T.J. Reid wouldn't have. That's a fair weapon to have. Tony is probably physically not the strongest wrestler, but his speed is a huge plus. He can hurl left and right, but another great quality he has is that he gets on the end of a lot of balls and finishes them well. He'll get the ball, break two or three tackles to finish off a great move – some of those scores are outrageous.

But because he's more of a finisher, I think T.J. Reid is probably the best I've ever played against. T.J. doesn't even need to be a finisher, strictly speaking, because he can win his own ball, high or low. He wins puckouts and makes scores, his work rate is top class – look at the number of hooks and blocks he gets through in a game. He's strong enough to turn his opponents over and bring his team-mates into the game. Then there's his free-taking. Tony Kelly was hot and cold in 2022 with his free-taking but T.J. never seems to have an off-day, and he's reliable up to 100 metres from the opposition goal. He misses so rarely, he's won tight games for Kilkenny over and over again. I don't know how you could argue against him as a player, which is why I have him as my number one. He has so much quality, you could play him in any position from midfield up and he'd make a difference because of that work rate and class. When you have those two attributes you can't go wrong.

But in fairness, Tony Kelly is very close! Speed is a fair advantage Kelly has, even if it's not uncommon at senior inter-county level. You get used to fellas with serious speed, but the odd time you'd see some lad and think, *This guy is at a different level.* Cork have a lot of speed in their forwards and they use it well, particularly for puckouts. If you have the likes of Robbie O'Flynn, Conor Lehane, Shane Kingston lined up in the middle and then they break to different parts of the field for the restart, it's a challenge – none of them are slow and it's nearly impossible to pick the right man to track.

One player who rarely gets mentioned when it comes to speed merchants in hurling is Richie Power, who was very hard to handle. Richie had great hands and real power, no pun intended, but he was also very fast, which is incredible when you consider the knee injuries he suffered during his career. Which brings us to that Kilkenny team of 2009 to 2014, when they could put out a forward line which gave you problems in every position. Henry, Richie, Richie Hogan, T.J., Eoin Larkin … The funny thing that time was that we didn't go out to man-mark them. We went out and played our positions as named and took up the forward who came in to mark us. Why would you man-mark Henry Shefflin if you also had Richie Power or Richie Hogan to contend with? Where would you start? They were so good that you couldn't make specific plans for one or two lads, you had to take them as a whole, and hope that every one of us was on top of our game.

As the years went on Kilkenny probably didn't have the same absolute quality in their forwards as they had between 2009 and 2014 (they couldn't have, some of those lads were among the best forwards of all time). When we played Kilkenny in 2016 and 2019 we were up against a forward line with Richie Hogan and T.J. Reid and thinking, *Maybe T.J. needs more minding than the rest of them*, because the likes of Richie Power and Eoin Larkin were gone.

One of my most difficult opponents was Johnny Glynn of Galway. He got two goals off me in one game and was very hard to handle, not just because of his strength, but also his sheer size. He's well over six feet tall and the long arm reaching in around and over you was very hard to manage. The irony is that I always preferred marking big players, like Walter Walsh or Henry Shefflin. I always backed myself to win the ball over them or beat them to the ball, but Johnny was really awkward. He's left-handed like myself, which made it even trickier, but he was just so rangy you couldn't get a grip on him. Another player that comes to mind is Aisake Ó hAilpín, though he mightn't have had the hurling Johnny had. With Johnny he had a hand like a telescope, it would stretch in past you just when you thought you had the ball in your own hand.

Then there was Henry. He's a big man physically and was never afraid to get stuck in or to confront anyone physically – but what set him apart was an unbelievable cuteness. For instance, he'd read in me when I was starting off that I was eager to impress, obviously. A young lad mad keen to make a name for himself, mad to win every ball – he noticed that early on, and he played on it. In that first five minutes of the league final in 2009, my first spin with him, I was mad to win an early ball, clean up the breaks, show everyone that I was there on merit and going to hurl all before me. To dominate. Henry had two points scored before I could blink, though, because he had that all figured out beforehand: *Here's a new man who's expecting a big confrontation, so what I'll do is slip in behind him and get an early point or two – and then his head is turned completely because instead of concentrating on his own game, he has to think about me.* I did manage to get into the game and get on the ball, and he had to change his game and come out to put me under pressure, but he'd started well. That was a lesson for me.

That confrontation was more physical than anything, by the way. I can never remember any lad really mouthing in a game. There would have been times against Kilkenny over the years when I would win frees coming out with the ball and they would have been shouting at the ref, 'He's diving, he's diving.' Now, at times I felt I had to exaggerate the action a bit because I wasn't getting the frees, and I wouldn't have got them otherwise, but I can remember Henry Shefflin often saying that I was diving, obviously to put the referee under pressure. But you're coming out with three or four lads dragging out of you – to me you're entitled to win a free on the back of that.

But in fairness during my career I can't remember a time when anyone was really in my ear mouthing off. If you crashed into someone and they said to f— off, that was fair enough in the heat of the moment, or in a bout of pushing and shoving. That's different. You'd hear plenty of stories coming out of Gaelic football, lads with the phone number of their opponent's girlfriend written on a wristband – they're great stories, but I don't know if they're true or not. I certainly never encountered anything like that in hurling, it doesn't seem to exist.

Maybe it's because of the speed of the game. Even when the ball is down at the other end of the field you both know it could be dropping down on you a second later, so psychological warfare isn't a starter. I could mouth off at an opponent but if the ball lands in a second later you hardly have the punchline out. Wrestling on the ground for 30 seconds? Often happened. Getting into your head with the verbals? Never did.

Maybe the referees in hurling had something to do with that, even if you always had a gripe with one or two of them. At inter-county I felt Barry Kelly was always fair and square. He was straight, he was even-handed, but one important thing was how he treated players. He might say, 'Pádraic, that's enough now, enough of that,' and you'd get on with it, but with another referee you might ask them why they'd made a particular decision and it would just be, 'Go away.' Barry Kelly would give a reason why a free was given – grand, and everyone got on with it. With a lot of newer referees there'd be nothing like that – if you asked why a free was given you might get the wry smile and the hand pointing in the direction of the free. That's very frustrating for players. Barry treated you like an adult. Even Brian Gavin, though we'd have been on the wrong side of a lot of the games he handled, would at least treat you like an adult. Sometimes in games down the years I encountered referees who had me thinking, *I see you have something on your shoulder saying, 'Give respect, get respect', which is fair enough, but doesn't that work the other way as well?*

I know referees have a tough job but if you ask a reasonable question – What was that free for? – and you just get the wry smile, or get dismissed, it's very annoying. You feel like the referee is putting you down, when the likes of Barry Kelly or Brian Gavin would have said, 'Pádraic, you pulled him, you know it,' and that was fair enough. Fergal Horgan is still good at that. He'll say to you, 'Pádraic, you know what you're doing, you know you've been pulling at him the whole time: free in,' compared to other referees just staring you down when you ask a question. I appreciate they have to deal with a lot of nonsense – even Brian Gavin had to deal with his nose being accidentally split open by Tommy Walsh in an All-Ireland final – but at times a few of them don't help themselves. Give respect, get respect – it works both ways.

Nine to five: work, hurling and the thin blue line

The life of an inter-county hurler or footballer isn't always straightforward – their working life, that is. People can sometimes have the notion that hurlers and footballers are taken by the hand and walked into handy jobs, ones which accommodate the commitments of their playing careers.

Not in my experience!

I was working away with a plumber here in Thurles about 2007. I was 18, and at 18 who's thinking long-term about their future? For me at that stage hurling was everything, my complete focus. When I was working at the plumbing for about a year, I was thinking, *I don't mind doing this, the job suits me.* So I signed up with FÁS, the whole lot, in 2008 as an apprentice, and I was officially working as a plumber for 2008, 2009, 2010. That was fine, and I was only 19 or 20 years of age at that stage and it was very convenient in that all the work was based around Thurles.

I was living at home in Thurles, we trained with Tipperary and the Sarsfields in Thurles, so it was very convenient, my timetable was very handy. I finished work on a Monday evening, then straight into the gym: I didn't even have to go home. It was ideal. The same then with training on Tuesday, Thursday and the weekend. Obviously the weekends were off anyway, but Tuesday, Thursday, finish work at 5.30, training straight away, or go home, get a snack, come back in to training. It was very convenient compared to the distances a lot of lads had to travel. Some of the work could be tough, a lot of lifting and dragging, but I was young, so it didn't bother me.

Then the recession kicked in. Coming up to the back end of 2010, the work got scarce – so scarce it was noticeable.

I didn't get a chance to finish the apprenticeship because I had an unappealing prospect ahead of me – to start moving outside of Tipperary for work or up to one of the other towns up the country. But that didn't suit me, and I wasn't prepared to do all that travelling. I was thinking, *If I start doing that, I'm not going to be able to play hurling properly.* You'd be travelling all day – leaving at half five or six in the morning and no chance of getting back til whatever time that night. I decided not to carry on. One or two other opportunities came up – people did offer me jobs in different places, but again, it didn't suit me to move away if I wanted to play for Tipperary.

I remember getting a phone call from a club in Dublin about transferring up, that I'd be looked after with a job, the whole lot. But to me, leaving Thurles would have been madness. I wouldn't have been able to do the work and all the training, including the gym work. Liam Sheedy was manager at the time and he was expecting a lot of us. I wanted to be right for the team, so in 2010 I packed in the plumbing. I was at a loose end at that point, but I was living at home so my running costs were low enough, at least. By 2011 I had been playing well with the county for two years, and with winning the All-Ireland in 2010 there was a bit of a buzz about the new players on the scene – a lot of us were getting 'gigs' here and there and I was basically living off that kind of occasional work. When I say gig I mean launching something or opening a supermarket, for example. Players get paid for those kinds of events, and with the high profile we had with Tipperary at that time there were enough of them going on to keep you afloat. Well, afloat if you were single and living at home with no mortgage to pay: that kind of 'afloat', but it's not a living, that's for sure. I remember in early 2011 going on the Late Late Show to talk about how GAA players, some who played in front of 80,000 people in Croke Park, were struggling to find jobs at the time.

By then I was turning 22. I hadn't a decent wage coming in and I was relying on those things to keep me going. But on the other side of that, I was young and I was there to train fully and concentrate on the game. I was a professional without being paid, really. I was going to the gym on a Monday and to the pool after that for recovery, training with the team on a Tuesday and I was able to go to the pool again afterwards. I'd just recover on Wednesday, do as much or as little as I wanted to do, and then Thursday the same, Friday, Saturday, Sunday the same. It was the constant routine of a professional athlete that you'd never get to follow if you were working full time, and I did get in unbelievable shape, I was feeling the best I ever did. And that year, 2011, was certainly one of my best as a player. I was flying it.

But that doesn't work long-term. While it's grand for a year or two, your mind then gets buzzing.

Behind it all you're not living the life of a professional athlete, for the most obvious reason in the world: you're not getting paid to do all that work. You need to have a job. Cian O'Neill was the strength and conditioning coach in 2011 with Tipperary, and he's a lecturer in that field – he's head of that department now in MTU Cork – so he'd be all over that area, really well informed about courses. He was based in the University of Limerick at the time and I was interested in one-year courses in health and fitness. I saw there was one in UL so the obvious thing was to ask Cian about it, and he encouraged me and helped me to get enrolled. I enjoyed UL and studied there for the year, which brought me into 2012, and the end of the academic year around May, which is also the Cúl Camp time of year. Parents recognise the Cúl Camps as a chance to get the kids out into the fresh air for a week or two every summer, but for inter-county hurlers and footballers who don't have full-time jobs there's a different association – it's a handy job for the summer.

In 2012 I was going to the camps all over Tipperary and was kept busy with that, and I was getting expenses. Out in the fresh air during the summer, a bit of coaching and having the craic with the kids. Ideal. But come that winter I had no job, so I was relying once more on a gig here and there. But we were getting such a good run at the club, and I was captain, I was feeling great, I was hurling very well, so I said, *This is suiting me now, I'll keep going with it*. My hurling was benefiting, certainly, because I was playing well, but in the grand scheme of things I needed to get back on track. And Eamon O'Shea, who came in as manager in 2013, advised me. He put it to me straight: 'Look, you need to start searching for something else, for a proper career.' I wouldn't be one for college – a lot of the lads obviously went to college and got the four-year degree, and more in some cases, but I wouldn't have had any great interest in going to college and doing something academic. I'm not built that way, and the older you get, the harder it becomes to chop out three or four years. I told Eamon that the college option wasn't for me.

Now, he's a very successful academic, he's head of the economics department in NUIG, but he's also a practical man. He got me a job with the water meters, which at that time were being installed around the country. I was based up in Kildare, just outside Kildare town, and the boss up there was a Tipp man, so he looked after me, in fairness. I was working in the store and in the office, looking after all the orders for the meters. I was doing that for a year and a half and I didn't mind it: the travel up and down was 50 minutes each way, so it wasn't taxing. I was up there at eight, I was home at half five. There was no pressure once I got my few bits done. I was left to my own devices, so I was happy enough. It was grand.

I did that and it stretched into 2014 and a bit of 2015 but, it wasn't a long-term career. That came from my mother, Helen. She had always pushed the guards, for some reason. I can remember sitting above in Kildare when a notification came up on my phone about garda recruitment. *Feck it*, I said, *I'll apply for it anyway*. So I put together my application and sent it off. In time I got called for an aptitude test and I got through that; then I got called for a second aptitude test and got through that. Then after a third series of written tests up in Dublin. Before I knew it, I was called for an interview. I was still going with the flow, to a certain extent, but I knew it was getting serious so I did my interview prep. I went to meet a few people to get some pointers on the interview. Then I did the interview itself, and made it.

It didn't happen overnight. This rolled all the way

through 2014 and into 2015. At the time there were a lot of people going for the guards. After doing the interview, there was a delay and I heard nothing for months: 2015 gone. Then early in 2016 I was called for a fitness test and a health screening. I got through that and finally got word that I was on the list and waiting to be called. But in early 2016, I got the note: starting in June at the Garda College. So it was only a matter of biding my time until then.

At that stage I hadn't really considered what the job would entail. By the time I was going in I was nearly 27 so I said to myself, *It's about time I started to look down the line, further than my hurling career.* And I would have spoken to a few lads who play hurling and who were involved in the guards, and they said, 'Look, it's great. There's great security, there's great benefits associated with being in the force. Obviously, the shift work can be tricky but if you work hard, you might get into an area that will help the hurling for a year or two.' They always stressed the positives of joining. For me it was just an abstract thing, rather than the practicality of calling to people's houses if they'd suffered a loss through an accident, for example, or making an arrest. I wouldn't have thought about all of that or realised how extreme the job could be, what was really involved.

The GAA being what it is, there were plenty of

connections in the Garda College. Eoin Cleary, the Clare football captain, was in my intake. So he would've been the same as me in terms of training and playing commitments. And I was there when Ken Hogan was in the college, when Eddie Brennan was there. There were a load of 'Ga' connections in the college and they were all brilliant to me. And I was glad to get in there by then, because in 2016 I didn't work from January to June. I knew this was coming, the garda intake, so it was very hard to look for a job and tell an employer that you would be gone in two or three months and that in the meantime you'd also be heavily involved in training with Tipperary.

In that sense, I wasn't a great employment prospect – why would an employer take on someone who'd be gone a couple of months later? I was picking up bits and bobs of work here and there to keep me going. Sars manager Tommy Maher was very good to me in that respect, finding jobs for me the way he did for others. But to be honest I didn't mind, because I knew I'd be starting in the Garda College in May, so I decided to train like a dog until then and be half professional. And I did. I had a great year, one of my best.

The Garda College was very handy too, in terms of location – I could be in Templemore from Thurles in 15 minutes. I was in the college for eight months. For the first three months a recruit is living in the college, but at five o'clock I could leave, go home, go training, go to the gym, so long as I was back that evening by 11. So for those first three or four months we stayed in the college Monday to Friday, and went home at weekends. After the first three months more people are coming in, so in order to accommodate those, the earlier recruits are put into digs around Templemore.

Out of 200 people in my group there were six or seven of us who were local enough, so we put in an application asking if we could stay at home in the evenings. That suited the college and it suited me down to the ground, because I'd be at home for training. It gave me a routine: get my own food, sleep in my own bed, the whole thing.

The training went well, and in February 2017 we were attested, as they call it, in the college. All of my intake were called into the big hall and the superintendent of the college was up in the front making the announcement: 'These are your stations.' This is a big moment for people. You've got new gardaí there who have families, kids, and the announcement is going to change their lives for the next few years at least. If you're a new garda from west Cork or Mayo or Donegal and you hear that you're going to be stationed above in Dublin, that's life-changing. Obviously we all know you could be stationed anywhere in the country, and to be fair to the garda authorities they'll listen to people making a case that they're from one place and they don't want to live 200 miles away, but they can't accommodate everyone's wishes. They'll try and not send you to Donegal if you're from Cork, for example, but sometimes there's no option. That's why there's fair tension when those postings are being called out; your life could literally change in the space of a few minutes.

The superintendent went down the line that day making the announcements. What was in my head was that he's a Clare man and big into his Clare hurling – a very serious man in a lot of ways but able to knock a bit of craic out of a situation when it suits him. So he came down the line and went down the list until he came to my name: 'Pádraic Maher' ... and a pause while he looked across to the list of stations ... 'Letterkenny garda station.' I was in shock. I was just sitting there dazed while he went on down the list, calling out the next three or four names. Everyone near me knew my situation and they were enjoying it, nudging me and chuckling away. I was trying to take it in, thinking, *He's not messing*, and then he stopped and looked up, smiling: 'Oh sorry, I read that wrong. Pádraic Maher, Henry Street garda station, Limerick.' I exhaled: 'Jesus.' And everyone started laughing. And the super said, 'I can hear that,' and carried on with the names.

It's funny now but that would have been an end to the hurling, really. Getting from Letterkenny to Thurles just wouldn't be a runner. If it happened, if you were posted somewhere that far away, you might not get back to your home place, or near it, for two or three years. It's hard, but you have to be posted to where you're needed, not to where it's convenient for you. That day people were probably posted to the opposite end of the country from where they were born and raised, so I was lucky. Limerick was decent enough, considering I was still less than an hour from home.

Being a garda has changed me personality-wise, certainly. That doesn't happen until you actually get out into the community day in, day out. It's funny how some people have this perception of the guards, that they're sitting down with the McDonald's, or the Supermac's, or the donuts. That's so far from the truth it's not even funny. I knew, obviously, what I was joining and what scenarios were possible. In the college, they train you for these possibilities and bring you through mock-up events. But it's not until you actually go out and you are thrown in at the deep end that you start to learn and realise what's involved. Obviously you go to the first few incidents, be it a horrific accident, or a domestic situation in a household or a drug issue, and that's when you realise this is actually more than a job: *I can't just come in here and dilly-dally around with these people. This is people's lives.* If they're having a serious family issue or someone has died tragically in an accident, or been murdered – nothing prepares you for that. You could be changing someone's life, when you knock on their front door. You may have to tell someone that a loved one will never come home, and you know that nothing will ever be the same for them after you knock on that door. That makes an impression on you because of course the first thing is that you put yourself in their shoes: what if it was you, or your own mother or father or brother in that situation?

I think it's definitely made me stronger as a person. You have a different outlook on life. Obviously in your own life you have to live in a certain way too, in that people don't know me now as a hurler, they know me as a garda. If you're a journalist or a carpenter or a plumber, that's one thing, but there's something fundamentally different if you're a garda or a nurse or a doctor. You're defined by your job, essentially. Experience helps, as it does in all walks of life. Once you've been through one of these situations, if it's happened once or twice, then it becomes second nature. You'll be sitting in the back office in the station on the computer, thinking everything is rosy, and next thing the phone rings … you'll be called out to a suicide, or to a person who has mental health issues, or to a murder.

I would have found it very hard to go into the job as a 21- or 22-year-old, without that much experience in life. But the fact that I was 26, 27, I'd gained a bit of experience by then and had been through some ups and downs. I had that base. But still it only prepares you for so much. It gets way more extreme when you experience it. I still wouldn't change it, though. Through all that heartbreak – the tragedies, the difficult issues to deal with – you can still get that sense of making a contribution, of maybe helping someone through a tough time. That helps, the sense that you're not just there in a nine-to-five job, and then home in the evening. You probably have to follow up with someone the next day after a major incident, and the next day, and the next day. There's a chain to it and you can't just switch off and tell them, 'It's half five now, I'm off, you're on your own.'

Does it make me appreciate hurling more? It does. Tipperary were beaten by Cork in Semple Stadium in May 2017 in the first round of the championship – we were All-Ireland champions at the time and I was in my first year as captain. And for the couple of days after I felt like it was the end of the world. *How are we going to turn this around?* Next thing I was in work and was called to a serious incident, life-changing for the person involved, and I was dealing with that for two or three days. The match was put in perspective pretty fast. I was thinking less about the end of the world in hurling and more along the lines of, *You know what? I get to go back training at the weekend, that's the thing to be grateful for.* We take hurling seriously, very seriously – but it has its place.

After a couple of years I was appointed as a community guard covering Moyross in Limerick. That's another strand to it – you see what people go through in their lives, how some are deprived of certain things. And then you see the other side – you help someone in the community, or the community comes together or organises something to help itself. You can see the positives even when things are going badly for people, how they can be hugely supportive of each other and band together to overcome obstacles and challenges. And that is a very inspiring thing to witness.

Roasting: opening a coffee shop

Over the years coffee became a big part of our preparation and relaxation for club and county games, and eventually part of my work life. If you'd told me that back in 2006, I'd have laughed, but it says something about Irish society as a whole, I suppose. We're a long way from a cup of instant coffee heaped with sugar.

Killing the day before a big game was always a challenge for us, and over the years we got into a routine. Maybe a bit of stretching, or a few pucks in the ball alley, and then a few of us would meet up for a coffee on the Saturday afternoon. It was ideal. You're with lads who understand whether you want to chat about the match or not because they're in the same situation, the environment is laid-back, and you're not sitting around the house with the prospect of an All-Ireland final in your head, draining away your energy.

After the All-Ireland in 2019 and early in 2020 we often met up in Thurles for a coffee, myself and Séamus Callanan and a few more, and eventually it came up in conversation that there was an opening for a coffee shop in the town. Now, at first we just said it as a joke, the idea of me and Seamus making coffees and serving them, but the more we talked about it, the more the idea of opening somewhere stuck. We ended up saying, 'Hang on, is there an opportunity here for real? Could we open our own coffee shop?' Séamie said he'd like to try it, and I said the same. He was in business anyway, working for Clancy Construction, so he had a fair amount of know-how, and I knew the town. We said we'd give it a go.

Great timing, of course, because Covid hit not long after and the whole country shut down. But we didn't stop thinking about it, and we noticed that there were coffee shops and coffee trucks opening all over the country, and that brought it home to us that the pandemic didn't necessarily mean the end of the idea. At the time there was really only one coffee place in Thurles. We made a few enquiries and got in touch with the Gaelic Players Association for some direction in terms of business development, and that was very helpful. The GPA immediately laid out the process for us and we discussed the idea with Ian Reeves, a development coach with the GPA. Ian was very helpful because he quizzed us about the whole thing: Why did we want to open a coffee shop in Thurles? Did we see the business being beneficial to us? Did we see it developing over the coming years? All valid questions that you need to have an answer for. Then he gave us homework, for all the world – things we needed to address – before moving to another stage. We spoke with Ian and his team again the following week and they put us in touch with another contact in the GPA as regards the financial side of things, the basics that we'd need to have in place for accountants, all of that.

In fairness, the GPA basically ran the development of the business by pushing us to organise our information, our documents, our plans. And they were pushing us – have this done by next week, or have that organised the week after, and so on. They were constantly on us, right up to the day we opened the door, and in fairness they came back and rang us after, and they called down to the shop to make sure everything was alright. It was unbelievable, the support; after that I was thinking, *Why didn't I use them more over the years?* They were unreal.

We eventually opened Heyday Coffee House in Thurles in October 2021, so at least the pandemic restrictions were easing by then. Of course we both have our full-time jobs. I work shifts – four days on and four days off, and when I'm on for those four 12-hour shifts, I'm pretty much gone. Whenever Séamus is working, though, eight to five or nine to five, Monday to Friday, if he's driving past he can stick his head in the door and make sure everything's alright. And the weekends he's off he can do likewise. My four days off could be at any time, so when I'm around I can pop in and out as well.

It's interesting. People are quick to say there's great money in it but it's like any other business – there's a lot of work involved and, to be honest, there can be a fair few headaches on top of your own job and whatever extra-curricular things you've going on – Séamus is still playing inter-county hurling, for instance, which is a fair commitment. It's busy and you're always on the go. It's your own business so you can't be opting out. There's constant discussion between us – I'd say if you went back over WhatsApp messages for the last two years you'd find that we've been in touch a few times every single day: there's always something that must be ordered, something has to be paid. There's something to do with accountants, something to do with the bank. There's always something.

But it's a great experience as well. It's certainly been an eye-opener to see what it takes to run a small business. It's definitely not something we regret doing, even though I still wouldn't be the greatest at putting a leaf on the top of a latte: my foam art needs a bit of work. I remember reading about an inter-county manager who said he heard players talking in the dressing room about the coffee being very good in one spot and not so good in another spot, and he was thinking it was all code for beer until he realised it really was coffee they were discussing. People don't understand how important coffee can be to inter-county hurlers and footballers, and not just for the taste. As I've said, it's a way to relax before a game – the foam rolling and then the coffee. It's also a bonding exercise, a distraction. You sit down to shoot the breeze and after a couple of coffees two or three hours are gone, and the bond is stronger again with lads you're going to war with 24 hours later.

And there's a little coffee trick we sometimes used as well. When Gary Sweeney was involved in our nutritional preparation he was an unbelievable asset to us – an incredible nutritionist whose knowledge and advice around food changed completely how I thought about it. In fact the way he made me understand food probably changed my life. He noticed I was drinking a good bit of tea and coffee, and on his advice I tried a slightly different routine. I had my last cup on the Monday of the week of a game if the game was the following Sunday. That meant no caffeine from Tuesday to Saturday. That was hard going for someone who'd drink tea and coffee by the gallon. Gary would say, 'If you want to have something, maybe have one green tea.' And that was it. So on the Sunday morning I'd wake up, have my usual breakfast but still with no tea or coffee. Then when we met up for the pre-match meal I'd load up on the caffeine. It gave me a great lift after a fair hard week. The Saturday used to kill me because I'd be having a green tea or a bottle of water, but all the time thinking, *Tomorrow I'll be having that coffee.* And during the pre-match meal on the Sunday I'd see Gary coming down to me with a couple of lovely Americanos – even though everyone else was making do with a filter coffee.

Whether it was physical or mental, the boost was real,

getting those coffees. If you're drinking a lot of coffee, giving it up feels like another sacrifice, but that's part of it too. You end up with a mindset of, *That's one of the few treats in the week of a game, having a coffee, and now I'm denying myself even that.* But you can turn that back on itself too: *I'm making this sacrifice to play for Tipperary and I'll get the benefit of it on Sunday. Is the man I'm going to be marking making the same kind of sacrifice?*

People might think that's over the top (I agree it sounds a bit mad, a little extreme) but it worked for me. At the top level it's often about giving yourself a chance to put those little bits of motivation together, to get yourself absolutely perfect for the big day. And coffee – even a lack of it – can help.

The devil is in the detail: the small print of hurling at the top level

Discipline is important, but experience is the key when it comes to getting the best out of yourself.

In 2012 we played a county semi-final on a Sunday, won it, and were facing the county final the following weekend, a gap of just one week. As we were leaving the stadium after that semi-final win I was already stressing to myself the need to be on top form for the final: 100 per cent, no excuses. Because of that I did a full running session the morning after the game. Up on a treadmill, flat out for an hour. With the result that I tore a muscle in my calf and was barely able to walk. All that week I was in with the physio, John Casey – who was also the Tipperary team physio at that time – and the day before the final I had to face into a fitness test to see if I could run. Up and down the hall in the clubhouse, sprinting back and forth, to show I was fit enough to play.

The next day I could barely get through the pre-match warm-up, but when the ball was thrown in the competitive instinct took over, and adrenaline got me through the 60 minutes. But I spent a few days on crutches afterwards because of the pain. That's experience. When it came to training I felt I ticked a lot of boxes in terms of commitment and application, but the first bit of advice I'd give to a youngster starting out, someone of 16 or 17, is simple: enjoy it. There are different elements to that, of course, and one is to ask plenty of questions – about everything. Nutrition, strength and conditioning, all the elements of preparation. The enjoyment comes from realising your potential and maximising the return from your preparation. Remember, there are metrics and measurements to tell you how efficient your preparations are. Good coaches will improve you and show you why and how you're improving as you go. If you do a one-rep max bench press one day and then follow a good programme for six weeks, you'll see an improvement in that one-rep max bench press the next time you do it. The same with speed tests and body fat measurements. Those results show the improvement and there's no arguing with them.

As I went on through my twenties I came to appreciate that even more. I took those tests seriously and reaped the benefits, and those who didn't, didn't get those benefits. That's a crucial lesson to share with the youngster who's starting out: if you start as you mean to go on you'll reap the rewards later in your career. Your attitude changes as you get older, obviously enough, because *you're* getting older. An older player advised me to keep an eye on my workload as I pushed on into my twenties, because I'd get more out of my performance if I stayed fresh rather than killing myself by going too hard in training.

That's a fair point, but there's another side to it – as you get older and the younger players are coming in, you feel the need to do that bit more in order to stay level with them at least. That sets off another circle again in that the older player has to do more to recover. I found myself taking more ice baths, stretching almost every day of the week, getting a massage twice a week with Mick Clohessy – I looked after myself far more because I had to. A younger player might head home after training and throw himself across the couch for the evening – something I often did when I was younger myself – because he can get away with it.

Between different training methods and extremes of nutrition I was always looking for that edge. I could see the benefits I got from Lukasz, our former strength-and-conditioning coach, and Cairbre Ó Cairealláin who is the current strength-and-conditioning coach with Limerick. Cairbre brought me to another level physically and also in recovery and preparation. He was unbelievable for me in the few years he was with Tipperary.

Mentally I always looked to find something extra as well. In early 2020 I shot Alan Quinlan a text – the former Munster star is also a Tipp man. I asked him could he arrange a little sitdown and coffee with Paul O'Connell, to see could I pick his brains.

Within a half hour the meeting was arranged. I wanted to speak and learn from the best, and anything I could do to improve my training, preparation, leadership, I was happy to do.

I met with Paul and had a great chat for over two hours one afternoon in Limerick.

Just even listening to his experiences, things he picked up along the way, how he overcame obstacles, disappointments, the winning of moments big and small, organisation, standards. I learned so much from him in that two hours – he was immense. He explained about people concentrating on the big things in life while forgetting the little things that add up to making the big things – the pebbles, he called them. I also learned our experiences weren't dissimilar.

I always felt I was at my best when I was given responsibility and leadership roles. Be it captain of my club, captain of Tipperary, vice-captain, part of leadership groups. I felt it brought the best out of my game and that my standards around training and prep were at a level others needed to reach. Maybe I felt that in the past few years, both with Tipp and Sars, I didn't get the same opportunities to show these qualities as I did in my earlier career. Lead by your actions, the rest will fall into place. I always felt I did that.

I wouldn't be big into collecting gear. I have some nice bits from playing inter-county but in general I wouldn't have held onto much stuff. That said, I have my All-Ireland and Munster final jerseys, and the Sarsfields jersey from the year we won the Munster club championship. I often gave away jerseys after games to charity, for instance, but not the All-Ireland final ones. Apart from one – at the final whistle in the 2014 All-Ireland final I met up with J.J. Delaney and swapped with him; his Kilkenny jersey is at home. None of my jerseys are framed or anything. You don't see them when you walk in the door, but they're well minded.

So are my medals. Like every other hurler and footballer in Ireland, I'd say my mother has all the medals I ever won, all my All-Star awards. They're in one small room in the home place along with Ronan's. I think his display case is more prominent than mine, but at least my stuff isn't in a biscuit tin!

I still have plenty of hurleys in the house, even though I'm not playing anymore. If you opened the hot press, plenty of them would fall out (Claire is driven mad when she opens the press and hurleys fall everywhere still; 'You don't need them anymore!')

I'm giving the club a dig-out with training sessions and I always have a hurley with me, even if it's just to hit the ball back out to lads who are taking shots on goal. If they were short for a drill that's non-contact I'd stand in as well, no problem. One weekend they were doing a wall-ball session and one of the groups was a man short; it was non-contact so I fell in, there was no issue – I had to show them how to do it properly!

Starting off, I'd go to Littleton for my hurleys, to John Ryan Moore, but when I fell in with Tipperary, Eoin Kelly introduced me to the Dowling hurleys in Kilkenny, which were lovely. I really like the ash, the feel of them, and used a lot of those. When Ronan started making hurleys obviously I used his because they were so good. I always used a 35-inch, with a bit of weight in it for the strike, but as I got older I switched to a 36. My logic was based on being in the full-back line, where every last inch could come in handy if you were trying to get a block or a hook in.

The helmets are still at home as well. I had a yellow Cooper for a long time, then that broke in a match, unfortunately – a league match in Ennis. Ronan Curran, the Cork hurler who's with Mycro, got in touch with me after that and gave me a few helmets over the years and I wore them. Back to the white Cooper for the last couple of years.

I might not be out on the field anymore but I'm still hugely passionate about hurling. The game's been very good to me over the years and I'm always looking at ways it could improve, ways to raise standards. Take refereeing: inconsistency might be a cliché but the way games are handled can vary widely, and it's definitely an issue.

You play a Munster semi-final and it's refereed one way, then you're in an All-Ireland final a few weeks later and it's handled in a completely different way. Take the 2022 Munster final between Limerick and Clare. Everyone felt that was a classic, and it was helped hugely by the way John Keenan refereed it – he allowed the game to flow and the players responded.

As I've said, some referees don't have a rapport with the players, which doesn't help, but I acknowledge absolutely that the level of analysis of every game is insane, and by analysis I mean the attention that's drawn to every tiny incident that happens on the field. Maybe it's because of social media, the fact that everyone has a camera and a platform available to them, but the game is analysed to a minute degree. Someone always catches something, and then there's a debate on it, but if there's a debate about absolutely everything, how can there be a focus on the important things?

To give the referees their due, they're also working to directions and to assessors, and those directions can change over the course of a season, never mind a couple of years. You'll often see that early in the year referees might be blowing for every dodgy hand pass, which is fine – but then come the championship and the need to let the game flow, and those hand passes aren't policed at all! What happens is you have one season being played under two different sets of rules. The players haven't changed their approach, but the referees have – and they don't get to communicate the fact that it's changed, on top of all that. Almost every year there's a different interpretation or another rule being thrown on top of them – black cards, yellow cards, lads pulled down inside the 20-metre line – while they're trying to keep an eye on the time, to track the scores … that's a heavy workload with 40,000 people roaring for your blood.

Outside of the refereeing, over the course of my career there's been a change in what's acceptable and what's not. I don't know if the shoulder I hit Joe Canning with in the 2016 All-Ireland semi-final would be seen as legal now. I know at the time there was no suggestion even of a free, but now I'm not so sure. There's a huge emphasis on protecting players now, which I fully support (unsurprisingly, given I had to retire because of a neck injury). But while protecting the head is absolutely necessary, are players changing the way they play because they don't want to go anywhere near the shoulders, because of the risk of a red card? With that in mind, I don't think the game needs two referees either. People seem to forget that in the big games there are two umpires at each end, two linesmen and a fourth official.

Would another pair of eyes make a difference if all those people are doing their job?

When I take my seat at Semple Stadium now, I see a different game to what I played starting out. The battle for the middle of the field, the short hand passes to players coming off the shoulder ... it's only now from my perch in the stand that I can see how it's changed. The senior hurling I started off with in 2009 has been transformed. That transformation was inevitable: Cork had changed the game when I came in and Kilkenny responded, Tipp made their contribution with the movement up front, and by the time I finished up Limerick had changed it all over again. Until someone finds a way past them that style will dominate for a few years yet. The suggestion that you just bypass Limerick in the middle by delivering the ball long doesn't stand up to scrutiny – with the likes of Diarmaid Byrnes and Declan Hannon they have players who can send the ball back with interest. But it does bring up the whole topic of the ball being too light, which I often hear people say.

If they're comparing it with the sliotars that were used 50 or 60 years ago, they might be right, but I don't accept that today's hurlers are hitting the ball too far. I can go back to 2010 when Brendan Cummins was able to score a free in the All-Ireland final from well inside his own half, so are players now hitting the ball a lot further than their predecessors? I don't think so.

The other evidence for the impact of the light ball seems to be high-scoring games, which baffles me. Aren't those high scores showing off great skills? Not every score comes from the other side's half of the field or a free 100 metres out.

Now, if people got half as worked up about the yellow ball … That really irritates me. Why are we playing with a yellow ball? What's wrong with the white sliotar? I remember Patrick Horgan saying it wasn't just the colour, he said he felt it played differently to a white ball, and I think he's right. To me that's a small change for the sake of it.

The future:
for me, for Tipperary

The cliché is that you finish hurling and because you've given your entire life to it for years, suddenly you have more time on your hands than ever. What I found was that after a couple of months I was wondering how I ever found time for hurling, given all the normal, everyday commitments I had: *How do people get the shopping and all the other errands done, never mind train or play on teams?* When I was playing, my whole life revolved around hurling, and everything else was put on the back burner – and I mean everything. Family commitments, even plans with Claire to head away for a weekend, all of those were dependent on my commitments to hurling. When I stepped back, then they became realistic options, which was great but inside I was struggling to adjust to life without hurling.

The routine is everything to an inter-county player. You know where you're going to be on any given evening – training this night, gym that night, a match this day, back on the field the following night. Then it's gone, that structure. And I found that challenging. At the very start I downed tools and stopped going to the gym (though I've got back into that more recently). Then I decided to give long-distance running a go, something I hadn't done while playing, and I ended up doing the half-marathons in Limerick and Cork, which were enjoyable enough. But the novelty wore off there too. For one thing, you're on your own doing the training, and when you've been involved in teams all your life that's another adjustment to be made. In team sport you're meeting people all the time and you're always involved in a group – going to games together, meeting lads in the gym to do a session, training. There's a whole bunch of people all working towards one goal, and even when training is hard there's banter between lads to lighten the mood. Adjusting to the lack of a collective is hard enough, particularly when I couldn't even fall back into the club. You realise that when the lads are organising something together because they're still very much part of the group – and you're not. Your family and friends are still there for you but when you leave the team environment, a huge part of your life is gone. You can feel very alone and isolated. You could be busy all day with work or seeing friends and family, but then something will remind you that you're not going down to training that evening, you're not involved with the club anymore. Sometimes it hits like that.

That change in lifestyle takes adjustment. When I'd just finished, for instance, I found that I was going to the pub more often with lads that aren't involved in teams. There's always a reason if you want one, 'There's a game on the telly, we'll head out and watch it', and I found myself having a few pints more often than I was used to. That was another novelty that wore off fairly fast, even for a Leeds fan like myself, suddenly free to watch the games over a beer. (Sheedy, Mick Ryan, Darren Gleeson, Dr Peter Murchan, John Tierney from the Tipperary Supporters Club, Nicky English – they're all Leeds fans, so there's a fair cohort of us hiding in the Tipp camp.)

Regrets?

A few.

I'm relatively happy and feel lucky to have got all I did from my career. I met so many great people and shared the dressing room with great men, I won many honours and saw many places in the world, but there are regrets. The 2009 All-Ireland final and how it finished, having been so close. The Munster club semi-final in 2016 against Ballyea in Ennis, when we were three points up with time gone only for Gary Brennan, the Clare footballer, to get in ahead of me for a ball from a sideline. He ran through and buried it to draw the game, and we subsequently lost in extra time.

The following year in the Munster club, against Ballygunner in Walsh Park, we felt we were the better team, but in the first half Pauric Mahony hit a long free into the square, where I was on the goal-line. I jumped to catch the ball and dropped it into the net. Again we were beaten in extra time.

My time as Tipperary captain was another regret, especially 2018. In hindsight, when players were leaving the panel, the mood around certain panellists, I could have helped and dealt with that better. Players need to look at themselves at different times but I could've done more when I was the leader.

My last act as a player was giving away a free in the last seconds of the 2021 county final against John McGrath. My health wasn't good then, as it later turned out, but giving away that free, John scoring it to end the game … that was my last act on a hurling pitch and unfortunately it'll probably never leave me.

My biggest regrets, though, are probably off the pitch. I received so many well-wishes, phone calls, letters, emails from so many people in Tipperary and outside the county when I retired but I also received them through my whole career, young and old sending letters and messages, and I never got back to them all. People were putting an effort into sending me a letter or an email or a card, and over time a few would have slipped away from me in terms of replies.

I regret that because I appreciated that support – from Lorrha to Clonmel, Nenagh, Thurles, Tipperary Town, Cork, Dublin, Belfast – everywhere.

I just wish I could have responded to all of those messages.

Of course, I wasn't the only one to call a halt this year: Brian Cody finally retired as Kilkenny manager. For the last few years you'd be thinking, *Would he not just go at this stage?* but you'd also see that he was getting something out of the players. Being straight, they didn't have the same quality of player that they had when we were facing them, but they were still able to win Leinster championships, to win All-Ireland semi-finals when nobody expected them to. This last year, again, he got Kilkenny to an All-Ireland final against the odds – they mightn't have played as well as they did in the semi-final, and maybe Limerick didn't let them, but they were within touching distance at the finish. And Cody was getting the most out of what he had. Maybe that was the ideal way to go out, on the back of a performance like that. The man transformed hurling, the way they performed and the standards they set. Even for us in Tipperary, with Kilkenny you were always thinking of Brian Cody, that dominant presence on the sideline. And he had that presence on the sideline, believe me. You could hear him in a match, the odd roar – that would make you stand up straight as an opposition player. There was never a comment to me or to any opposition player as far as I can recall. There'd be the odd bark at the linesman or the referee, but apart from that he was always on to his own players – and always encouraging.

I'd say if you were a Kilkenny player and he was there encouraging you in a big game, you'd grow ten feet tall, and that stemmed from his career, but he backed that up. You'd often hear stories that the Kilkenny players aren't that close to him, but on the pitch every one of them went out and died in their boots for him and for Kilkenny. Fair enough, a lot of the older players give the impression that even now they wouldn't be that close to him, but what counts is what they did on the field for him – and they did everything they could to win, which shows the respect they had for him.

We had that respect for him too. Win or lose, he'd be over to you. If we won, it was: 'Well done, ye deserved it', and if they won, it was: 'Hard luck, ye gave it everything, no regrets.' There was never a sneer or a grin – the only time I ever saw him laughing was after the drawn All-Ireland in 2014, when he said, 'We'll see ye again in a few weeks.' He transformed hurling. The standards he set in Kilkenny set the standards for every other county.

I'll be one of those trying to match Cody's standards, it turns out. At one point during the summer I was in the gym, Xtreme in Thurles, when the Apple watch started to buzz. Liam Cahill. He'd just been appointed Tipperary senior manager after a whirlwind 24 hours, replacing Colm Bonnar. I stepped outside to take the call, expecting him maybe to be looking for a steer on lads, a bit of a pointer or two. When we spoke, though, he cut quickly to the chase. He and Mikey Bevans, the coach he works with, had been chatting and they wanted me to get involved with them on the management side with Tipperary. I was surprised, but my initial feeling was one of excitement – butterflies in the stomach – because it was the closest you can get to playing yourself.

I met Liam and Mikey that evening for a good long chat. They told me what their plans and ideas were, and I was impressed – but I told them I obviously needed to speak to Claire and my family, because it was such a big commitment. Being a selector is almost more time-consuming than playing, because as a player you're only looking after yourself and your own preparations, whereas in management you have to keep an eye on everyone and everything. I spoke to Claire and she was a great help, pointing out that even though we were trying to organise our wedding, it was really too good an opportunity to pass up. 'We've a lot going on but this isn't something that comes to everyone's door, particularly this fast,' she said. Along with my gut instinct, that sense of excitement, I'd also had the experience of watching Tipperary play in my first year of retirement, and I obviously wanted to help in whatever way I could.

I was back to Liam within 24 hours and said I was happy to come on board. And typical Liam, he put me to work immediately. It seemed like only yesterday that I got a phone call from Liam Sheedy inviting me in to the Tipperary senior panel, but it was winter 2008. Another evening phone call, but in summer 2022, and I'm starting off all over again with Tipp, just in another role. People have asked me if it's too early – I've played with a lot of the lads, I'm friendly with them, Ronan is involved – but I think the players will appreciate that anything I do will be for the good of Tipperary hurling. I don't care who isn't playing and who is playing, we'll be picking the strongest panel we can to get the best out of them for the county. Watching the lads not win a championship game in 2022 and not get out of Munster – we don't want that to happen in 2023 and I think the players will respect what we'll be trying to do. I'm friendly with the lads and I'll continue to be friends with them but we'll all understand what we're there to do.

Our best for Tipperary.

Acknowledgements

Thanks to all the people who made my story readable and enjoyable (I hope). I never thought in my wildest dreams I'd ever write a book about my life, and I've tried to be as open and honest as possible.

First I want to thank my parents, Paddy and Helen. What you have done for me in life, let alone hurling, has been incredible, same for Ronan. The constant support and sacrifices, always the best for me and Ronan in mind. Everything hasn't been straightforward for us but we've come out fighting the other side. No words here will do you justice. Thank you both.

To Ronan, thanks for always being there through the good and bad times. Through it all we have had a great relationship and will continue to do so, along with plenty of craic. Enjoy the rest of your career, make the most of it and have no regrets. I have no doubt it will continue to be fantastic.

To my family who have been such a constant support to me, my uncles Paddy, Maurice, Dinny and Connie – you all were an inspiration to me over my career; my aunts Catherine, Judy and Mary you were and continue to be great supporters of Ronan and me. I hope we did you all proud. To all my in-laws and cousins, we are such a tight family, you were in my thoughts every time I put on the jersey. Thank you all for your support.

To my new in-laws, Claire's Mam and Dad, Jean and John, and her sister Emma, thank you so much for welcoming me into your family, I can see why Claire raves about you all so much. Thank you for your support also. Even if it's from Clare, I'll take it.

To everyone who helped, guided and supported me in Durlas Óg, Scoil Ailbhe and Thurles CBS. I wouldn't have had the career I had without your help. I have so much gratitude for what you have all done in my career. Thank you.

To all the lads in my club Thurles Sarsfields, thank you so much. We had some unbelievable days, days people can only dream of. We put in a enormous amount of hard work but by God did we enjoy it all, both on the pitch and off it. We had plenty of tough days away from the pitch also but most importantly, we stuck together to this day and have come out the other side, stronger than before. I can't really put into words what the club means to me.

I have been so lucky to get the opportunity to wear the famous blue and gold jersey of Tipperary. It was only a dream of mine, but to make it a reality – the days of both success and disappointment I will never forget. To all the great men I shared the dressing room with, the backroom teams, the Tipperary county board, the Tipperary Supporters Club, thank you for memories that I will bring to my grave. It was a privilege to play for and represent you all.

To Liam Sheedy, Declan Ryan, Eamon O'Shea, Mick Ryan and all your selectors, coaches and backroom staff, you all had a massive influence on my life and to you all I am so grateful for the opportunities you gave me. Thanks a million lads.

To Michael Moynihan for all his help (and to Marjorie, Clara, Bridget, Bobby and Breda for helping him to help me). I probably drove you around the bend on many occasions but in the end I hope it was all worth it. You were a privilege to work with. Thanks again. Gent.

A special mention for Eddie O'Donnell, the man that makes it all tick. Never anything left out or taken for granted. Fair play, Eddie – thanks for everything.

To Ciara and all the gang at Hachette Ireland, you made this so easy for me and Michael and were always a constant support to me during this. I hope it does you justice.

To my colleagues in An Garda Síochána, at both Mayorstone Garda Station and Henry Street Garda Station – there are so many that I can't name everyone. It's a privilege to serve with you, and thanks for the help and support over the years.

To all my Sars supporters and Tipperary supporters, there have been plenty of ups and also many downs. It has been a roller-coaster but I hope I have done you proud throughout the years. You were always a constant and brilliant support to me. That will stay with me forever.

Finally, to the most important person in my life, Claire. Sorry for driving you mad over the last few years. I hope you could see and understand my reasons for doing so. I look forward to making up for it all in the future. I love you so much and cannot wait to see where our journey brings us.